Considering the apostle Paul's teaching, it's much easier to believe "Jesus' grace is sufficient for me" than "Jesus' power is made perfect in my weakness." How is it that my difficulties, hardships, and persecutions can be a good thing? Jay Hewitt reveals God's upside-down way of working in our lives and enlightens us by showing how God's supernatural ability is beautifully displayed in our natural inability. Run to the Strength Giver without delay.

KYLE IDLEMAN, senior pastor of Southeast Christian Church
and bestselling author of *When Your Way Isn't Working*

Far more than being a beautiful expression of Jay Hewitt's life, this book reveals the beauty of being human. We tend to forget that to be weakest in the flesh is to be strongest in God's Spirit. Jay's vulnerability powerfully illustrates what it looks like to lean into Jesus in the darkest of times. If you're looking to learn more about being resilient and trusting God in the dark, I highly recommend this book. It will make you laugh and cry, and it will also provide helpful tools for trusting God when you don't understand his ways. Jay's integrity and willingness to keep learning what it looks like to trust Jesus have encouraged me in my own walk with God. This book will not disappoint!

CHRISTY WIMBER, author, pastor, former TV host, and current
director of global church planting for Friends Southwest

Jay Hewitt is one of my heroes. At the age of thirty-seven, this amazing husband, father, and pastor was diagnosed with terminal brain cancer, yet persevered with a deep faith. Jay's story touched my soul deeply. What he has learned through his journey is a powerful reminder that your circumstances may not always change, but your attitude can change—and that makes all the difference. His life story is pure inspiration.

JIM BURNS, PhD, president of HomeWord and author
of *Doing Life with Your Adult Children*

Jay Hewitt has chosen to bravely reveal intimate details of the journey he and Natalie have been on for the last several years. I'm proud of the ways God has moved, shaped, refined, and empowered them during this triathlon-sized challenge. It's impossible to read this book and not be moved to tears. As you let Jay's story soak in, you'll see that you can have the same power Jay has. He is a good man, a great husband, and a remarkable dad. In this book, he shares his amazing and powerful story of freedom, joy, and healing. Anyone facing an IRONMAN-sized challenge will love this book.

PAUL ALEXANDER, PhD, president of Hope International University

As a functional medicine practitioner, I've seen inexplicable peace and joy exude from people going through the most challenging times in their health. Jay Hewitt highlights this concept and shows us that hope can always be found. Leading with practical guidance, he explains exactly how we, too, can walk through life with an unshakable resilience, no matter what is thrown at us.

DR. WILL COLE, leading functional medicine expert and author of *The Inflammation Spectrum* and the *New York Times* bestseller *Intuitive Fasting*

When confronted with the most difficult of circumstances, Jay Hewitt answered the call of his heart to alchemize his challenges into a higher purpose—to inspire! This book will do just that—inspire you to live a more purpose-filled life.

JOE HAWLEY, former National Football League center

ZONDERVAN BOOKS

I Am Weak, I Am Strong
Copyright © 2023 by Jay Hewitt

Published in Grand Rapids, Michigan, by Zondervan. Zondervan is a registered trademark of HarperCollins Christian Publishing, Inc.

Requests for information should be addressed to customercare@harpercollins.com.

Zondervan titles may be purchased in bulk for educational, business, fundraising, or sales promotional use. For information, please email SpecialMarkets@Zondervan.com.

ISBN 978-0-310-36747-5 (softcover)
ISBN 978-0-310-36749-9 (audio)
ISBN 978-0-310-36748-2 (ebook)

All Scripture quotations, unless otherwise indicated, are taken from The Holy Bible, New International Version®, NIV®. Copyright © 1973, 1978, 1984, 2011 by Biblica, Inc.® Used by permission of Zondervan. All rights reserved worldwide. www.Zondervan.com. The "NIV" and "New International Version" are trademarks registered in the United States Patent and Trademark Office by Biblica, Inc.®

Scripture quotations marked GW are taken from *God's Word*®. Copyright © 1995, 2003, 2013, 2014, 2019, 2020 by God's Word to the Nations Mission Society. All rights reserved.

Scripture quotations marked MSG are taken from *THE MESSAGE*. Copyright © 1993, 2002, 2018 by Eugene H. Peterson. Used by permission of NavPress. All rights reserved. Represented by Tyndale House Publishers, Inc.

Scripture quotations marked NLT are taken from the Holy Bible, New Living Translation. © 1996, 2004, 2015 by Tyndale House Foundation. Used by permission of Tyndale House Publishers, Inc., Carol Stream, Illinois 60188. All rights reserved.

Any internet addresses (websites, blogs, etc.) and telephone numbers in this book are offered as a resource. They are not intended in any way to be or imply an endorsement by Zondervan, nor does Zondervan vouch for the content of these sites and numbers for the life of this book.

All rights reserved. No part of this publication may be reproduced, stored in a retrieval system, or transmitted in any form or by any means—electronic, mechanical, photocopy, recording, or any other—except for brief quotations in printed reviews, without the prior permission of the publisher.

Published in association with the literary agency of WordServe Literary Group, LTD, www.wordserveliterary.com.

Cover design: Micah Kandros
Cover photo: Andre Gie / Shutterstock
Interior design: Denise Froehlich

Printed in the United States of America

23 24 25 26 27 LBC 5 4 3 2 1

I am Weak I am Strong

Building a Resilient Faith for a Resilient Life

Jay Hewitt

ZONDERVAN BOOKS

To Natalie—
I am so in love with you

Contents

foreword

In his book *Reaching Out,* Henri Nouwen tells the story of a former college student who returned to his alma mater and slipped in to watch Nouwen teach again. After class, the former student invited his old professor to lunch.

"Dr. Nouwen," the former student said near the end of the conversation, "when I'm with you, I feel as if I'm in the presence of Christ."

Nouwen smiled. "My son, it's the Christ in you who recognizes the Christ in me."

I've known Jay Hewitt for more than half of my life. We met in college. He was in charge of our dorm floor, back when I was just a kid with an improv punk band and a dream to become a pastor someday. And he was up for any adventure, absolutely fearless, a lover of people and God's Word, and just one of those people who had a rare ability to make any moment deeper or wildly more fun. In many ways, we grew up together—learning who we were and who we wanted to be, making mistakes and growing from them, developing our identities, and cultivating a deep and abiding faith in Jesus side by side.

I left my time with Jay always wanting to connect more deeply with Jesus. I think that's why I love Henri Nouwen's response—"it's the Christ in you that recognizes the Christ in me"—because I recognized something so different about the way Jay chose to live. He made me want to be better. He is special. He listens, makes room, meets you where you're at, allows for honesty and challenge, and offers words of encouragement and support. I've always thought of Jay as the friend who would always have my back.

When he called to tell me about his diagnosis, I was devasted. I remember being at a total loss for words, my mind and heart struggling to keep up with the information I had just received. How could Jay, such an intense and brilliant person, be facing the vulnerability of humanity at such a young age? I thought of his wife and his daughter, of all the dreams and ambitions that could shattered by such a loss, and then I wept. I vowed to stand by him and support him in every way I could, and in so doing, I've had the honor of a front-row seat to his pain and exceptional courage. He is definitely made of stronger stuff.

The Bible records a scene that beautifully displays the power of what can come from being pressed. Just days before Jesus' crucifixion, he stepped away from the public eye and headed to Gethsemane. His intention was to set aside time with a few dear friends who could hold space as he prayed and begged God to relieve him of his prophesied death. In other words, this was not a light meditation but more like a desperate plea for mercy. Luke 22:44 even says that Jesus' emotional agony was such that "his sweat was like drops of blood falling to the ground."

I had to know what it was about that specific garden that made it the setting for such a dramatic scene. Had it been a special place for him before? Was it particularly holy ground? Was it just a quiet, out-of-the-way place? When I learned that Gethsemane comes from two Hebrew words that together mean "a place for pressing oil," I was in awe. Olives are pressed in order to make olive oil, which was a precious commodity for the culture of the day. Imagine massive baskets of olives being crushed under an enormous weight, precious oil seeping out into clay jars to be stored, sold, and used for ceremonial purposes.

Everything Jesus did was intentional. Believe me when I tell you he was signaling by his choice of Gethsemane. He was saying something about grief, fear, and faith. He could have easily changed his mind and backed out of his divine commitment to death, burial, and resurrection (though there was no guarantee the resurrection would even happen). We'd be hard-pressed (see what I did there?) to find fault in a man who refused to go into a situation that ensured a torturous, horrific death. He could have gone into hiding, living out his days as a carpenter somewhere where no one knew his name. And yet when Jesus was pressed to the point of blood under the extreme stress of his pending march to the cross, his choice was to accept his path and submit to the future God asked of him.

I've often thought of Jesus' agony at Gethsemane as I observed my friend Jay. In the midst of intense fear and uncertainty, as he was pressed and crushed under the weight of his possible future, he showed us who he truly is—a man overflowing with the fruit of the Spirit. Time and again—through his work, his life, and his words—Jay, even as was being pressed, exudes more love, joy, peace, patience, kindness, goodness, faithfulness, gentleness, and self-control. I've always wondered how he did it. One day as we hiked together amid massive ponderosa pine trees, he told me how 2 Corinthians 12:8 had transformed his mindset.

What you hold in your hands is a gift from a guide I deeply love, trust, and respect for how he has chosen to embrace the pressing imposed on his life. What could have crushed his spirit seemingly brought out the best of Jay Hewitt. The vulnerability with which he writes showcases his pastoral heart and puts on display the faith he embodies even during the most challenging moments of his life. Whether you're currently walking through an unimaginable pressing of the spirit or are walking with someone who is, this book will encourage you, inspire hope, and pastor you as you face adversity head-on. May Jay's words inspire you to cultivate the kind of faith that when you're being pressed, crushed, or stressed allows for the best fruit to come forth from your one and only life.

Steve Carter, author of *The Thing beneath the Thing*

Prologue

"Why me?"

At the age of thirty-seven, I was married to an incredible woman and raising a beautiful three-year-old girl. I was leading a growing, vibrant, young Southern California church when the bottom dropped out on me. "Why me?" was an obvious first question after being handed a frightening diagnosis.

Terminal brain cancer.

"Why me?"

From that very first moment in the late spring of 2017, I have been processing and testing and adjusting as I sought to understand the purpose of my pain. Each question led to more questions. I would not give up my search for understanding. Eventually I began to see more clearly how it's possible to be strong when weak and how to rejoice in suffering. The lessons God taught my soul have proven to be immensely valuable to me, and I believe this book will be equally valuable to you as you try to make sense of this crazy life. Are you seeking strength and resilience on the path to making your life count? Of course you are. But how? How do you become resilient?

I want to help you discover the answer to that question as I believe God has guided me. The journey starts by wrestling with God and your own self-doubt. You must be willing to ask hard questions of yourself and of God.

I assume that right now you are facing something challenging that requires resilience. There is always something, isn't there? Your thing may or may not be more difficult than my thing. But hard is hard, and I'm convinced we can all do hard things.

I'm also convinced that when hard times come, it's normal to ask yourself, *Why me?* But if you're going to ask that question, you also have to ask, *Why* not *me?* And if you're going to ask *why* when something tragic happens, then you have to ask *why* of the good stuff of life as well.

Why am I the guy who, in my midthirties, was diagnosed with incurable brain cancer? I'm a pastor, which makes some people really struggle when they find out that I have a terminal illness. Their sense of belonging to a universe of ordered justice is challenged.

"Why do bad things happen to good people?" they ask.

I don't feel that as a pastor I should get any preferential treatment from the Big Guy upstairs, because I know all too well that holding the pastor title doesn't change my standing with God. I am no more righteous than the next guy—and God doesn't play favorites anyway.

But I do struggle with wondering why, after coming so far in my faith, God would let me get knocked down. Why, after making real progress in a lifelong battle with my own childhood trauma, would I get stopped in my tracks?

Since marrying Natalie in 2003, I've been confronted with the fact that having been grossly neglected as a baby created relational obstacles in my current nuclear family. Deep fear gripped my heart and held me back in many ways from moving forward with my own family. I was terrified of having a child of my own because I felt so ill-equipped. After years of therapy, I finally found enough emotional healing to recognize that it was possible to access the internal resources I needed to be a competent father. The decision to have a child was especially scary for me, but it was a fear I wasn't willing to allow to stop me from moving forward.

Our daughter Hero's (Natalie is a professor of Shakespearean literature) birth felt like such a victory, a wonderful gift from the hand of God. Why, then, just three short years after finally having a beautiful baby girl, would I contract a terminal illness?

I fought so hard to finally become a father. It feels cruel to set up my daughter to lose her dad at an age when she will need me the most. *Why, God?*

But on the other hand, why not? A disheartening fate, yes, but as I cried out, I was forced to consider that I'd had more than my share of good fortune as well. It's impossible to know for sure if the good outweighs the bad or vice versa. But I can tell you that I've had some notably serendipitous stuff arise in life, and I believe there are more great things to come.

I'm the guy who got called down to contestants' row on *The Price Is Right* and won *a new car*! Three hundred of us had been waiting in line in front of the studio for hours. Six high school friends and I had spent the night before in a tiny room at the Farmer's Daughter Hotel across from the CBS Studios in Burbank. We got up at 6:00 a.m. and stood in line until 3:00 p.m. When the doors finally opened, two producers asked the same two questions to every single person: "Who are you?" and "What do you do?" Most people simply gave their first and last name and then stated their occupation. Only later would they realize that contestants' names *weren't* just pulled out of a hat—that, in fact, they were being interviewed for potential on-camera charisma.

My friend had been to the show before, and he was ready this time. When they asked him, he clearly stated his name and then told the producers he was a performer in a traveling circus, where he was famous for riding a unicycle with a bear. They didn't buy it, and they were clearly not amused.

I was up next. It was my eighteenth birthday, and I remember my answer verbatim as I poured on the charm: "I'm Jay Hewitt, and I'm currently waiting for my girlfriend to get home from a trip to South America. She's going to have some great stories, and I'm hoping to have one to tell her too." They asked me a few follow-up questions, and we all knew I was going to get called down. And I did!

Jay Hewitt, come on down! You're the next contestant on The Price Is Right.

Thanks, Rod Roddy, but this wasn't luck. I earned it. I nailed my interview. I had watched enough episodes to know that after they brought out the home-gym weight machine to bid on, because I had the last position, I would be able to either bid one dollar higher than the highest bidder or say the satisfying phrase, "One dollar, Bob!" I said that phrase with confidence—and won! So after nailing the interview and sticking to a time-honored strategy, I was soon onstage, next to Bob Barker, noticing his two-inch-thick stage makeup as he said, "You could win *a new car*!"

A stagehand peeled away a false stage door, and a Geo Prizm appeared. It was a terrible car. I knew because my mom owned one. It was 1999, and at the turn of the century, the Prizm was discontinued. (Two years later, the brand disappeared.) All for good reason. But it didn't matter. A free car is a good car, and there was no way I was going to win it anyway.

After showing off the car, Barker's Beauties brought out a slow cooker, a toy fire truck, and a mop. In order to win the car, I would need to know the prices of these items. I had no clue. As Bob explained to me how the game *Switcheroo* was played, I didn't hear any of his instructions. I just thought, *I don't want to look like an idiot on national TV.* The game started. I looked at the list of possible prices. Audience members were shouting things I couldn't understand, and I knew I had one option—guess. I randomly lined up the prices, switched them around so it looked like I was being strategic, and took a step back in the hope that I guessed correctly.

The whole experience was so overwhelming that I was completely flooded with excitement and behaving with zero reason. The next thing I knew, all the prices in front of me were lit up in a blinking green—and I had won a new car . . . and a mop! I had a little to do with getting onstage, but once there, it was dumb luck that provided me with a new car. I didn't do anything to deserve it. But I'd take it!

What percentage of the world's population has won a car on a game show? I wonder now if it's higher or lower than the percentage of the world's population of under-forty-year-old men who have been diagnosed with a grade 3 astrocytoma brain tumor and given six to ten years to live?

I don't know, and I don't care. All I know is that driving my new car in college helped me graduate debt-free with an undergrad degree, and I was so grateful that I gave the car away, hoping I could help someone feel as fortunate as I felt on that Burbank soundstage, on July 16, 1999.

Nineteen years later, a neurosurgeon showed me the scan of a new tumor on my brain and explained calmly, boldly, and directly, "It's brain cancer."

Why? Why would God bring me so far in my life only to have it all come crashing down with tumor recurrence and a cancer with no cure? It made no sense.

Frustrated, I cried out, *What are you doing, God?* And then, as I had experienced only four times before in my life, I heard the voice of God speak directly to me. It was not a booming voice like you might expect. It also did not resemble my own thoughts. Instead, it was a calming, reassuring voice that said, *My grace is sufficient for you, for my power is made perfect in weakness,* just as Jesus told the apostle Paul in 2 Corinthians 12:9. My mind instantly reached the same conclusion as the apostle reached in verse 10: "When I am weak, then I am strong."

This is my account of how I am weak, yet I am strong. This is my life. This is what it is to be human. You are weak. You are strong. Our stories are unique, but the same God is at work in you. You are about to learn how to find your strength within your weakness.

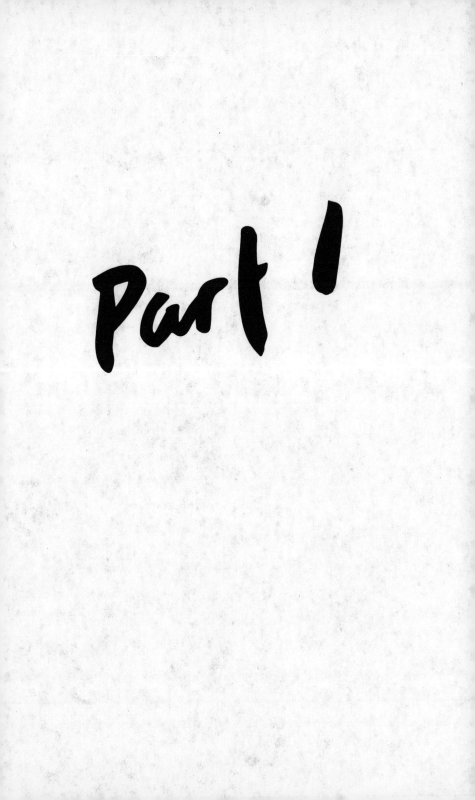

Part 1

CHAPTER 1

Round One

Everyone has a plan until they
get punched in the mouth.

MIKE TYSON

My favorite sport is boxing. I boxed for a couple years in my late twenties and was proficient enough to be a sparring partner for a guy who was turning pro. But I got a late start and had no delusions of ever becoming anything more than a punching bag for someone with a future in the sport.

I boxed at a gym in Westminster, California, called Grampas. It wasn't one of those cardio gyms that used punching bags as part of high-intensity interval training. Grampas was intimidating. The perimeter of the gym was lined with heavy bags, speed bags, and strength-training benches. It had an area where guys would work their abs and strengthen their necks. There was another area where boxers worked with their trainers, throwing combinations and focusing on footwork and timing.

Right in the middle was the ring. Even when a tournament wasn't going on, the ring was surrounded by spectators, including Grampa, watching guys spar. Grampa's granddaughter was a beautiful, up-and-coming Latina boxing star who routinely whipped on bigger guys—which everyone loved to watch. Fortunately, I never sparred her. My jaw was too fragile, and so was my ego. But as I mentioned, I sparred the soon-to-be pro many times and heard a lot of "ohhhhhs" when he snapped my head back with a stiff jab that led into a brutal combination and added to his highlight reel.

I learned a lot during my time at Grampas—a lot about angles, accuracy, and how to use my body to throw a punch. But by far the most useful skill I picked up was learning how to fight. More precisely, I learned how to not give up.

When you're eight rounds into a sparring match, with another four to go, each three-minute round can feel like an eternity, and the sixty-second break between rounds is just enough time to question whether you can keep going. You'd think it would be natural to keep your hands up in front of your chin to fend off that fist coming right for your jaw. But as you get tired, your hands get heavy and you don't even realize when they start to drop.

One thing that sparring with someone better than you teaches is to keep your hands up and not give up. The effort it takes to continue to fight is grueling and painful. Giving up hurts more than fighting. If nothing else, my time in the boxing ring taught me to fight for a full twelve rounds.

What I didn't know then was that fighting brain cancer is a lot like going the distance in a boxing match. There are many different types of cancers with different treatment paths. My particular brand of brain cancer is chronic—meaning that it never goes into remission. Some seasons will be more intense than others, but as I fight this kind of cancer, I never get to take the gloves off. I get short little breaks between each round of treatment, but they never feel long enough, and I dread starting the next round before I catch my breath and begin to recover.

In the early rounds of a boxing match, the fighters are learning each other's style and trying to figure each other out. It's the same with cancer. As I write this, I'm still in the early rounds and still learning.

My fight with cancer started with a quick knockdown. Long before my official diagnosis, I had returned from a trip back east and was tired. It was May 29, 2017, when I was walking into a meeting in our historic chapel that I felt strange. Instantly an incredible amount of energy hit me right in the gut and spread out in all directions—downward to my toes and upward to my head. When the surge simultaneously hit my legs and heart, I went weak, my knees buckled, my heart started racing, and I intuitively laid down on a row of chairs.

At first I thought I was having a panic attack, but the energy continued to move down to my feet and up to my brain. At that point I felt something I had never felt before—an out-of-body experience. It seemed as if I was hovering above myself.

I had a great sense of dread. I thought I was in danger. Although I was alone, I perceived a mysterious figure approaching who meant to do me harm. Feelings of nostalgia, déjà vu, and anxiety collided all at once. I was a conscious observer of all this, but I was not in control.

Several minutes passed before I returned to something like normal. I was exhausted. I rested for a minute and then got up and walked into my meeting. I faked my way through it and then called my primary care physician. Looking back, this Monday afternoon in May was the first time I learned I wasn't in a one-on-one fight; I was in a tag team match with no backup. I was about to get jumped by my health insurance company and a gang of incompetent doctors and specialists.

Tag Team

Just because someone has been practicing medicine for a long time doesn't always mean they got good at it along the way. The receptionist at my general practitioner doctor's office tried to schedule me for an appointment sometime in the following month. I pushed my way into an appointment later that afternoon. In the office of a general practitioner, I sat on an exam table, the white paper crunching beneath me as I described to the doctor what I had experienced. He told me it was just an anxiety attack. I disagreed. He sent me home with a prescription for antianxiety pills. He should have sent me home with anti-seizure medication. As a result, I had my second seizure the next day. It wasn't what I knew a seizure to be—unconscious, convulsing, tongue-biting. I now know what I just described is called a generalized tonic-clonic seizure. I was experiencing a different kind of seizure—one I had never heard of.

I knew it wasn't an anxiety attack, so I went back to my doctor the next day and told him his pills weren't working. He replied, "Well, it takes time." I pushed back. Finally he folded and said, "Fine. I'll refer you to a neurologist." A week later, after suffering ten more seizures, I met with the neurologist, who gave me a quick diagnosis without having any evidence for his hypothesis. "It's some scarring on the brain. No big deal. I see it all the time. But just in case, I'll schedule you for an MRI."

Two weeks later, after some frustrating miscommunication with my medical insurance company, I got my MRI done in a parking lot in one of those trailers that elementary schools use as portable classrooms. When I came out of that claustrophobic tube, a receptionist handed me a compact disc and told me to take it to my neurologist.

As I sat in my car, I took a quick glance at the disc and noticed the label read, "MRI of the uterus." *Um, what?* I took the disc back in and said, "This is not mine."

"Are you sure?" the receptionist asked.

"Yup," I said, "unless you've just discovered that I have a uterus."

He fumbled around and came out with a disk labeled, "MRI of the brain."

I took it to my neurologist the following week, who said, "Just as I expected, there is some scarring on your frontal lobe." With that incorrect conclusion, he dismissed me—still without any anti-seizure medication.

Finally, that Sunday at church, I mentioned my misadventures to a friend, Kevin. When he learned I had gone a month without the medicine I needed, he was intensely upset. Kevin is a former chief of police and FBI agent—the kind of guy you don't want to see become upset. He said determinedly, "You are being mistreated, and I'm not going to let this continue." It was like I had found my tag team partner and tagged him into the royal rumble. I mentored his son some years before and had been at his house praying with his family the day before his son underwent brain surgery to remove a benign tumor.

This was not Kevin's first fight, and he had my back. He offered to show my MRI scan to his neighbor Dr. Kim, a well-respected brain surgeon. I handed him the disc, not knowing what to expect. Later that afternoon, my cell phone rang. It was the brain surgeon calling me from his personal cell phone on his day off.

Dr. Kim said he wanted to see me in his office as soon as possible, and while my insurance wouldn't cover the visit, he said he would comp it for me. For the first time, I felt like I was talking to a medical professional who actually cared.

But then he delivered the worst news I had ever received in my life. "Jay," he said, "I'm looking at your scan, and you have a tumor in your brain about the size of a Ping-Pong ball."

How do most people respond in a moment like that? I went into problem-solving mode. I knew next to nothing about tumors, but just enough to ask two important questions:

Is it cancerous? He told me it appeared to have good boundaries, so it was possible it was benign. But that couldn't be determined by a scan.

Will I need brain surgery? He told me it appeared to be in a location that might allow for surgical amputation, but he would have a better look in his office when I came to his office.

"We can discuss options then," he said. The phone conversation was brief, kind, and insightful. It was also devastating.

I thanked the benevolent neurosurgeon and hung up the phone. Slowly I turned and walked upstairs to the bedroom where Natalie was putting on a dress she had just bought. With her back to me, she asked me to give her a hand with the zipper. In the soft afternoon sun, I helped her and then turned her toward me and gently said, "The neurosurgeon just called. I have a brain tumor."

We shared a look of shock and fell into each other and crumbled into the bed. The moment was tender. I held her close, her hand on my chest. Our daughter was quietly sleeping down the hall. I was surrounded by everything worth fighting for and everything I was afraid to lose. I was going to need them in my corner if I was going to fight valiantly.

Who's in Your Corner?

For a monumental fight, if you want to go the distance, you need something worth fighting for and a good team in your corner. Although at some point each fighter must step to the center of the ring on their own, your support team will determine the outcome of your solitary challenge.

I was caught off guard when life punched me in the face and knocked me flat on my back. But fortunately, I had a solid network of relational connections and people who truly loved me—people I could turn to when I needed help getting up and finding a way forward. Friends, congregation members, and family members all wanted to know what they could do, and they helped me develop a strategy for pulling in kindhearted people and positioning them to become effective members of my fight team:

→ Build a strong support team now by supporting other people in their struggles.

→ Find the strength and courage to let people help, starting with prayer.

Letting people help is harder than it seems. To ask for help is to admit that you're weak. But if you're facing your own monumental fight, then asking people to pray is a great first step—and it works. Anyone can pray. Even if they aren't particularly religious, they can send good vibes.

Some people will pray for you just one time, and that's fine. Others will have a deep concern for you, and you will naturally show up in their prayers on a consistent basis. The next time they see you, they'll let you know they've been praying. When you thank them for their spiritual support, be sure to share some details about what you're facing and what you'd like them to specifically pray for—a no-pressure way for them to help. I've found that as people pray for specific things, God's Spirit gets involved and guides them toward the realization that he has uniquely positioned them to assist in a truly helpful way.

At that point, people begin to offer help that goes beyond prayer. Some will, quite imprecisely, say, "Let me know if there's anything I can do to help." Others will offer some specific, unique offer that may be genuinely helpful. It's up to you to either take them up on their offer or just let it rest as a loving gesture. Either way, keep those offers in the back of your mind because in the future, you may need someone to watch your kid for the afternoon, give you a ride to an appointment, or help you find a lawyer—all examples of offers made to me for which I humbly came back to ask if their offer still stood.

Although leaning on someone is simple, it's hard to take the first step to ask for prayer. Asking for prayer is hard for me because it makes private things public. After my appointment with Dr. Kim, he sent me to get a better MRI scan. Three days later, I was in radiology, waiting to be called for a new and improved MRI scan. I was nervous, and right at that time I received a text from Connie, a member of my congregation. Although I may be one of her pastors, she is a lot wiser and more spiritually mature than me. Natalie and I weren't especially close to Connie, and we didn't talk to her too often. So I was somewhat surprised when, out of the blue, I got a text that read, "You've been on my heart, and I just wanted to tell you I am praying for you."

She knew nothing about my medical issues, and I was truly moved to know I was being supported in prayer. My immediate reaction probably should have been to thank her and tell her why her text meant so much to me. Instead, I sat there in the waiting room, staring at the words and wondering if I should mention how nervous I was to get this MRI and to find out the results.

I have a problem with not wanting to appear weak. I don't like to admit when I'm scared. I've built a reputation as a pastor for being *authentic* and *transparent* because, while onstage, I talk openly about the struggles and trials in my past. But I purposefully discuss only those issues I've already resolved because I never want to project my current unresolved challenges onto my congregation. I have since learned that not wanting to appear weak is itself a weakness.

Sitting in that waiting room, I was definitely in the thick of a trial, with no idea what was going to happen next. I felt too vulnerable to respond to a kind acquaintance's text with any meaningful information. After all, there are strict laws in place to protect people's medical privacy. That was my reasoning for deciding not to respond ... until I felt the Holy Spirit speak wisdom to my heart: *You can trust her, and people need to know so they can know how to help. You need help.*

I started typing, a long response divulging many private details. Rereading my reply, the feelings of vulnerability made me cringe. But I sensed that I had received divine wisdom I needed to follow. Despite what my gut was telling me, I went with my spirit and sent my message. Her response was simple and immediate: "You've got my prayers, friend." I could hear her nurturing voice as I read her words. That unexpected exchange started a chain reaction, first in my heart and then in a long series of God-ordained happenings. I started asking for prayer and telling folks they didn't need to keep the information private.

Dr. Kim, who had responded to Kevin's request and called me on a Sunday afternoon, soon put me in touch with another highly regarded neurosurgeon named Dr. Duma, who then connected me with Dr. Berger, a world-renowned specialist who was way outside of my reach.

As I sent out requests for prayer, friends and friends of friends rallied around my family in monumentally compassionate ways—countless home-cooked meals dropped at our doorstep, babysitters on call, and homes available for us whenever we had to travel for treatments. I found support in many forms—emotional, spiritual, marital, physical, and financial. My colossal fight requires a large team of strategists, cutmen,[1] and people compassionate enough to pick up the towel of service in some areas of life when needed.

Everything may be going according to plan for you right now. But be aware that at any moment, life can deliver an uppercut that will put you flat on your back. Don't wait to start surrounding yourself with people you'll want in your corner when you get hit by that punch you didn't see coming. The time you spend now investing in the lives of other people will have an incremental effect on the support available to you.

Don't wait for sudden bad news. Realize that other people matter. Their struggles matter. And when you need help, don't hesitate like I did. Let people know. Ask for prayer. Be specific. Take people up on their offers of support, and be courageous enough to take

---

1. A cutman is the person on a boxer's corner team who treats cuts, swelling, and other injuries by using abundant amounts of different equipment.

a risk and ask directly for help. The Bible clearly instructs us to "carry each other's burdens, and in this way you will fulfill the law of Christ" (Galatians 6:2). When you make it a priority to support others, you are building a support team for yourself for your times of need. Those you're currently praying for, walking alongside, and offering to lend a hand to—they're the ones you'll most likely find in your corner later.

I don't think it's a coincidence that it was Kevin who first stepped in for me and turned the tide when I was drowning. After all, he's the father of a kid I had once supported. There at Kevin's house the night before his son's brain surgery, I talked with his son Cody about how he was feeling. I gathered the family for prayer. I came around after the surgery for moral support.

I helped carry their burden because I truly cared. Unknowingly, I was creating a bond that would be critical to my care later on when Kevin gave my MRI to his neurosurgeon friend. When I called to thank Kevin for his kindness, he gently said to me, "We are brothers forever." He has been in my corner ever since.

What's your fight right now? Who are the people in your corner? Don't wait to build your team until life picks a fight. God doesn't want you to face the difficulties of life alone. It takes strength to choose humility, admit you are weak, and let people know you need help. Take a risk and ask people to pray for strength in your specific struggle. Look around and ask yourself, *Do I know of anyone who needs my support?* God has uniquely positioned you to help them in ways others cannot. When you are able, stand with those who need you. Don't be surprised to see them in your corner in the future.

The journey to resilience starts by wrestling with God and your own self-doubt. You must be willing to ask hard questions of yourself and of God.

---

1. What benefits come to mind by challenging your preconceived notions of God and his actions in your life? What do you think God may be inviting you to work on as you wrestle with these questions? I'm going to assume that right now you are facing something challenging that requires resilience. There's always something, isn't there?

2. If you consider yourself a naturally resilient person, where do you find strength to endure difficult situations? How do you typically recover from disappointment? If you don't consider yourself a resilient person, how do you typically get through difficult situations? Who or what do you lean on when your back is against the wall?

CHAPTER 2

Awake to Tell about It

Great stories happen to those who can tell them.

IRA GLASS

It's not always easy to find a medical specialist who is both competent and compassionate. It had taken me a month and the help of a friend to find Dr. Kim. On June 27, 2017, I met with Dr. Richard Kim. I was numb. I was still in problem-solving mode. I was on a fact-finding mission. I had no idea what I was walking into.

I arrived at the medical offices inside an impressive glass tower of a building and walked into the waiting room, where I checked in at the receptionist's window. It was early in the morning, the sun piercing brightly through the chilled air. Unlike my usual experiences at a doctor's office, I didn't have to wait long. I didn't even have time to gather my thoughts before Dr. Kim appeared with the temperament of a counselor and welcomed me back. I followed him into his office where he already had the scan of my brain displayed on the screen.

He got right to it, which was kind, because all I wanted to know was what I was dealing with. (I have come to appreciate doctors who go directly to the crucial information and forgo the usual niceties.) He pointed out a big white area in my brain and confidently said, "This area is your tumor. It seems to have good borders. There is a good chance that this tumor is not cancerous."

He paused and continued, "Yet brain tumors are never truly *benign*, but rather they are *precancerous* if left alone. Eventually, they will become cancerous. If the tumor is able to be amputated completely and the cancer cells haven't yet diffused throughout your brain, then it is possible that after surgery you will be given a clean bill of health and can expect a normal life expectancy. However, at this time there is no way to tell in a scan if cancer cells have spread throughout your brain or if they are contained to the visible tumor. Only time will tell." He concluded, "For the immediate future, there is one goal—complete amputation." Essentially, Dr. Kim was saying that it was very important to cut the entire tumor out of my brain.

"What's the likelihood of removing 100 percent of the visible tumor?" I asked.

"Hard to tell. But I'm not the right guy for the surgery."

That brought our time together to an end. The meeting was brief. I left with a list of possible surgeons and instructions to check with my insurance to see what kinds of treatments would be covered. I also left with a prescription for anti-seizure medication.

I had my first seizure in May. After suffering multiple seizures daily for a month, I finally had been given medication to treat the problem. To say Dr. Kim was kind to me is an understatement. He turned the tide for me. After leaving his office, I got on the phone with my insurance company, and the long list of recommended surgeons was significantly shortened to a couple guys whom insurance would cover. For the next month, I met with every single surgeon covered by insurance. Each surgeon said the same thing to me—"I'm not the right guy for this surgery"—and declined to take on the surgery.

The search for the right surgeon for my needs was hard and discouraging, until finally I found one who seemed promising. Dr. Duma was an in-demand neurosurgeon in Orange County. People came from all over the world to be under his care, and he was willing to meet with me. I had watched his TED talk and had heard of his awards.

I arrived at his state-of-the-art facility in Newport Beach, walked in, and hit the button in the elevator for the top floor. After checking in, I was taken to the corner office overlooking the vast and calming Pacific Ocean. The neurosurgeon was in a fine suit behind a grand desk. Before he said a word, I thought to myself, *This guy is good! This is my guy.* He put an image of my brain on a large flat-screen monitor. Looking up at the screen, I was frightened to see again the Ping-Pong-ball-sized lesion in my brain. But I was quickly emboldened by his confidence when he agreed to do the surgery. After having multiple surgeons decline to do the surgery, I was beginning to wonder if I was going to be told that my tumor was inoperable and handed a prognosis of a shortened life span. Instead, I left his office with my heart puffed full of hope . . . until the next day when he called and said he was not qualified for this surgery.

My heart deflated. I was deeply discouraged and got off the phone feeling lost. Dr. Duma called back an hour later, and for the first time I was made aware of the reality of my situation. He told me that part of my tumor was easily accessible through surgery but that another portion would be very difficult to safely remove. He reminded me that in my case, it was crucial that 100 percent of the tumor be removed. Then he told me that there were only five surgeons in the world qualified to attempt the surgery I needed. My heart sunk. Then he told me that one of those five surgeons' contact information was in his cell phone. After our last conversation, he made a call on my behalf and asked if his friend would take me on.

"Jay," he said, "book a flight to San Francisco for first thing tomorrow morning. I've arranged an expedited appointment with one of the top five brain surgeons in the world. If anyone can help you, he can."

I immediately booked a flight to San Francisco.

The Eloquent Cortex

The next morning, Natalie and I drove to the airport, jumped on the first plane out, and took an Uber to another state-of-the-art medical facility. We got in the elevator and hit the button for the top floor. We were shown to the corner office, which had a view overlooking the expansive Golden Gate Park. As we sat there, about to meet the seventh neurosurgeon in my journey, I thought to myself, *We'll see. Maybe this is my guy. Maybe not.* Just then, the neurosurgeon walked in. His presence was steady, unworried, and unhurried. He had an aura of kindness without being particularly warm. He introduced himself as Dr. Mitchel Berger, took off his white coat, sat down, and grabbed a model of the brain.

He got right to it. He explained that the tumor was on my right temporal lobe. The type of tumor was most likely an *oligodendroglioma*. Chemotherapy and radiation would have no effect. The only course of action was to remove it—all of it. But it wasn't cyst-like, so it couldn't just be cut off. It was infecting actual brain tissue; consequently, portions of my brain would need to be cut away. "But not to worry," he told me. "You'll function perfectly fine, even though you'll be missing a major portion of a temporal lobe. You might just have a little memory loss."

He told me it wasn't a big deal—that this part of the surgery would be easy to perform. However, the *entire* surgery wouldn't be easy—in fact, quite the opposite. The complexity came because the tumor wrapped down a small canyon between the temporal and frontal lobes and into the interior of my brain, called the insula or, as surgeons often referred to it, the "eloquent cortex." Surgically removing tumor-infected brain matter from this region was a high-risk procedure—a *very* high-risk procedure.

This portion of the brain is responsible for some of the more eloquent functions like movement, speech, critical thinking, emotion, recognizing social cues, applying an appropriate filter to your thoughts, and other elements tied to personality and social functioning. You know, basically the part of your brain that makes you a person. As you can imagine, a mistake when removing a portion of my eloquent cortex might have life-altering consequences. Just to make things more intense, the insula is guarded by many arteries, one of which is major. If that major artery were to be severed during surgery, I would suffer a stroke, which would result in complete paralysis, possibly even death. To safely maneuver his way past the artery to the tumor, the surgeon would have to perform the equivalent of Luke Skywalker's flight through the trenches of the Death Star to destroy the reactor core. (If all this doesn't sound sci-fi enough for you, just wait. It gets worse!)

Because of the difficulty of this surgery, Dr. Berger suggested he perform the surgery while keeping me *awake*. Crazy, right! If it sounds crazy to you, imagine what it sounded like to me. My face turned white as a sheet. I became sick to my stomach. I imagined what it would be like to be aware as a surgeon removed portions of my brain. I was afraid I'd have a panic attack and be trapped on the table with my head fastened in a surgical vice. The very idea felt like being buried alive.

Dr. Berger saw the color leave my face. "It's the safest way," he assured me. He said it would painless, that I'd be in a dreamlike state. He explained that by keeping me awake, he could probe my exposed brain with an electrode and ask me questions, determining how I'd be affected before he removed each tumor-infected portion of my brain. He told me not to worry. The brain has no pain receptors, and so I wouldn't feel a thing. He wouldn't even have to use anesthesia beyond simply lidocaine on my scalp.

He was supremely confident. Let me give you a bit of back-ground on Dr. Berger. Neurosurgery was not his first choice. Football was where he had expected to make a career. He played college ball at Harvard and was expected to go on to play in the NFL . . . until he got injured.

Neurosurgery was his fallback! How many football players headed to the pros could give up their athletic dream and pick up brain surgery instead? Not many, I'd guess. But his athletic back-ground serves his patients well. He is on an NFL board charged with figuring out how to mitigate head injuries. And when he walks into a room, standing at six feet, five inches tall, he commands attention. His presence gives a certain confidence even when you're about to face the scariest thing you could ever imagine. So all that to say, I was thankful for his confidence—and yes, I had a bit of a "man crush" on this exceptional human being.

I shared with him that I was worried. "What if I freak out during the surgery?" I asked. The thought of having a panic attack while strapped down to a surgeon's table with my head in a vice terri-fied me. "That has never happened on my table," he assured me. He further explained that they would knock me out at first while they opened my skull, and then when they woke me up, I'd still be in a heavily sedated state. Dr. Berger could tell I wasn't buying it, so he told me it was up to me. He could do the surgery with me awake or asleep, but he recommended that for best results, the surgery be done while I was awake.

"Let's schedule the surgery for a couple weeks from now, and that'll give you some time to decide." Shell-shocked, I thanked him for seeing me. We then walked out of his office to the front desk and scheduled my surgery for a few weeks out. Then we got on the plane, and I tried to shake the imagery from my mind as I headed home.

The moment Dr. Berger told me he wanted me awake during surgery, one specific scene from a movie popped into my head and would haunt me for the next couple weeks. It's the scene from the psychological horror film *Hannibal*, where the serial killer traps his victim, performs a lobotomy, sautés the removed portion of the victim's brain, and then feeds it back to the unknowing victim. I watched that horrific scene sixteen years earlier, and it was so traumatizing that I recalled it with precise clarity and detail as I sat in the surgeon's office and imagined myself in the role of the victim in my own horror film. And I thought to myself, *Why did I ever go see that? Oh, yeah, because I thought it would be funny.*

Yep, funny. I was a sophomore in college. It was Valentine's Day, and my bros and I thought it would be humorous to take dates to dinner and a movie . . . but instead of going to the usual romantic comedy, we'd surprise them with a thrilling and disturbing horror film that all the critics were saying *crossed the line*. Yep, I was a real dreamboat. I distinctly remember during that scene looking at my date and realizing that it was a bad idea. Then I looked at my best friend, who was trying to not puke. Like the tough guy I thought I was, I made fun of him in front of our dates afterward. The joke was on me. Sixteen years later, and I'm trying to keep my cool in front of my wife and avoid throwing up in a surgeon's office. I was trying with all my might to act like the suggestion of being awake for brain surgery didn't faze me. I wasn't fooling anyone.

I had a decision to make. Dr. Berger seemed like a smart guy, but it was ultimately up to me to give my consent to undergo surgery while conscious. I wanted to be confident of my consent, but I was nervous about being awake for surgery. So I did what you would do. I googled it! I stayed away from those sites that make the situation seem worse than it is. Instead, I read medical journals, which bluntly tell you how bad it truly is!

I found an article by Dr. Nancy Ann Oberheim Bush that addressed my exact medical situation. According to Dr. Bush, the stakes were high. As I read the article, I found confirmation of what Dr. Berger had already said to me. Seeing it in writing hit harder: *there is* no cure *for grade 2 oligodendrogliomas*. Whoa, seeing those two words—*no cure*—sent a shiver down my spine, and I realized I was dealing with a fight for my life. She explained, in similar fashion as Dr. Berger, that radiation and chemotherapy are not effective in curing this specific type of brain tumor. I started to come to terms with the fact that the only hope for a cure was to catch it early enough and achieve a full resection (amputate the entire tumor) or else . . .

Then in her impersonal, academic article, Dr. Bush shared information that other doctors had neglected to tell me . . . probably because they didn't want to get ahead of themselves: if any tumor remained in the brain, it would kill me within four years. Four years!

At that point, it was clear that the only way to survive this brain tumor is to cut it out completely. Dr. Nancy "Bad News" Bush, continued: "The feasibility of *full resection* [getting it all out] depends on the *location of the tumor*. . . . When the tumor is in the *eloquent cortex*, it is important that patients be treated in expert centers, where they can have '*awake mapping*.'"[1]

I desperately needed a full resection and my tumor was in the eloquent cortex—Dr. Berger was a specialist working in an expert center where he was a forerunner in the area of awake mapping within the eloquent cortex. The decision was made for me. It felt crazy to agree to being awake during brain surgery, but it would be even crazier to pass up the opportunity.

A friend stepped into the gap for me, got me to a well-connected neurosurgeon who got me an appointment with a highly sought-after, elite-level surgeon. I would be crazy to not see this opportunity as a blessing. I agreed to the surgery. I agreed to star in my own horror film.

It's amazing how freeing it can feel to make a decision. I had no

---

1. Quoted in Caroline Helwick, "Low-Grade Gliomas: Understanding the New Treatment Paradigm: A Conversation with Nancy Ann Oberheim Bush," *ASCO Post*, March 10, 2017, https://ascopost.com/issues/march-10-2017/low-grade-gliomas-understanding-the -new-treatment-paradigm.

idea whether the decision was a good one or not, and I didn't care. Once I had gathered the necessary information, I asked myself what I wanted instead of fixating on what I didn't want. At that point, the decision was easy to make. I wanted my best chance at surviving this tumor longer than four years. Of course, I didn't lose sight of how great a risk this surgery was going to be. I didn't want to have a panic attack during surgery or be an eyewitness to something going wrong, but I had no way of knowing whether either of those things would come to pass. What I did know was that if I didn't do the surgery awake, I wouldn't have the best chance of Dr. Berger successfully pulling off a full resection.

So I went with what I knew instead of dwelling on what I was fearing. And I found rest in knowing I had made the best decision with the information I had available to myself. Beyond that, I had no control. And I found comfort when I reminded myself that my God *did* have control. I focused on the comfort of Scriptures that offer encouragement such as, "Do not fear, for I am with you; do not be dismayed, for I am your God. I will strengthen you and help you; I will uphold you with my righteous right hand" (Isaiah 41:10). I was starting to see God's presence in multiple steps along this journey. So I took a breath and recentered myself on the one thing I knew I could trust—God.

As soon as one worry resolves, of course, another appears. I was no longer troubled by the thought of being awake during surgery. Instead I discovered something even more daunting. I found a study written by Dr. Berger in another medical journal. In the study, he was able to determine what percentage of tumor he would be able to remove, depending on the quadrant it occupied in the eloquent cortex. In my specific case, my tumor was situated in a quadrant that he could predict with almost certainty that he could safely remove only 80 percent of the tumor. I then read a peer review of his study that confirmed his predictions as accurate.

Eighty percent is pretty impressive, given the delicate area of operation—an area in which other surgeons would deem inoperable. But 80 percent is not what I needed. I needed 100 percent. My tumor has "no cure," so it's all-or-nothing. Perhaps leaving only 20 percent of the tumor behind might buy me a little more time than the four years that Dr. Bush stated. Regardless, to face such a high-risk surgery with an outcome that is expected to be less than adequate is, at best, unsettling.

Scared Yet Strong

When we are unaware of the divine help and supernatural strength available to us, we may find ourselves running from a fight we can win. I'm not talking about the situations where we psych ourselves out and create fear where there shouldn't be any. I'm also not talking about that cliché acronym False Evidence Appearing Real, which can shame us into overlooking real risks and doing things we ought not to do. I'm talking about times in life that are genuinely dangerous. Life-and-death moments, instances that can sink us or launch us, decisions that will alter the direction of the rest of our lives.

God wired our brains to use the emotion of fear to alert us to danger and threats. And yes, we must also use the parts of our brains that God wired to discern between real threats and unnecessary worries. Ultimately, many times in life we will face true danger and will appropriately feel afraid. We can be scared yet strong. However, we don't have to be strong and dumb.

First, we must assess the risk we are facing and decide to fight or to run. If we believe we're fighting alone, we will run from battles we could have fought and won. But God, who regards us as his children, is always with us (1 John 3:1). When we confront risk by accounting for both our own personal limitations and the divine assistance of an all-powerful, all-knowing Father God, we will be connected to a source of wisdom and valor that will sometimes guide us into situations that seem crazy but have stunning, victorious outcomes.

The Bible is full of accounts meant to inspire us to approach risk with the assumption of divine help. Take the book of Exodus, for example. God put a stranglehold on Pharaoh, king of Egypt, and forced him to grant freedom to God's people (Exodus 12:31). As is often the case, the newly freed people faced an entirely new set of problems. Although no longer in captivity, they also no longer had a place to live.

After a long and brutal journey through a resource-scarce wilderness, they finally made it to the place God had promised them—a perfect new homeland. The problem was that the land was already inhabited by those who most likely wouldn't be welcoming to squatters (Numbers 13:1–25). Oh, and compared to God's homeless wanderers, the established inhabitants were gigantic—in size, number, and military might. But in God's divine wisdom, he encouraged his people to be "strong and courageous" and to move in and take possession (Joshua 1:1–6). The vast majority of the displaced people decided it would be better to die slowly in the wilderness than to risk being violently killed in their new home.

Many of us live with this mindset. We'd rather tolerate a miserable status quo than take risks to bring about a better tomorrow. Fear of suffering a miserable failure can keep us in a miserable existence. In that case, we'll always have misery, even though we could have our hopes fulfilled on the other side of risk.

I know you have pain in your life. You also have hope to move past the pain. The way forward always requires risk. Risk carries with it the very real possibility of failure. As you assess the risk of embracing change, don't neglect to calculate the cost of staying entrenched. And please don't overlook the possibilities that come with following a God who is with you and who can do immeasurably more than all you can ask or imagine (Ephesians 3:20).

Within a generation, new leadership had arisen among God's people who dared to believe that if God had rescued his people once and led them to this place, then he could be trusted to make a way forward for his people once again. They inspired strength and courage in their people, and finally they moved forward. And yes, they were not welcomed with open arms, but with the very violence they dreaded. However, with divine help, they survived and eventually thrived as free people in their new homeland.

If you are suffering in an abusive relationship, stuck in a toxic work environment, or held prisoner by addiction, I know the situation you find yourself in is dire and complicated. I understand that change invites a new host of problems. I can recognize that the alternative to your current hardship may appear to be even more difficult and may threaten to be even more devastating. When you are assessing the options to figure out what would be better—to stay or to go—it may seem you don't have the courage to move on or the strength to face the retribution of your oppressor and rebuild from scratch.

Not knowing your exact situation, I'm not advising you toward one action or another, but I'd like to ask you to reassess your situation. Consider a new possible outcome with a heavenly Father who values you as his child and who has a reputation for making a way when there is no foreseeable next step. Learn to find your confidence and courage in the knowledge that you have access to divine help and supernatural strength. Spend time meditating on the reality of a benevolent God whose attention is turned toward you. Be patient, knowing that adopting a new, brave way of thinking takes time because, with the compassion of the Holy Spirit, a new script can emerge. Pray and ask for God's divine guidance to know if the time has come to move out of your home or position at work or current coping strategy and move into a new season of growth. Pray and ask for vision to see what could be. If you are led to move, expect to face a new set of problems. But also expect God to go before you, walk beside you, and have your back as you move on. Keep your preferred future within sight, and press on until you experience freedom.

⸻

Generations after God's people fled from Egypt, they developed into a legitimate nation called Israel. Like all legitimate nations at the time, they were surrounded by legitimate enemies. A neighboring kingdom planned an ambush on Israel, but when their plan was discovered, a prophet named Elisha was wrongly accused as a spy and an enemy. Military troops were sent to arrest him. Elisha woke up in the morning to a panic. Everyone in his household was in a frenzy because his property was surrounded.

Most people in this situation would make a futile attempt to flee. But Elisha gave the command to stay put. He was a man with a powerful connection to God, and as a result, he had the ability to see with spiritual eyes that he was surrounded not only by enemies but also by an even bigger army of God's protection. He prayed and asked that the others in his household would be given the same spiritual insight that had been given to him. Their eyes, too, were opened. Courageously, they stayed put.

When the king of Israel received word of the ambush, he planned to send in troops and destroy his enemies. However, Elisha's bold courage led him to bless instead of curse. Surprisingly, he prepared a feast for his enemies, invited them in, and then sent them safely on their way. In doing so, Elisha did not merely survive; he created a new alliance that allowed him to thrive in the future without fear (2 Kings 6:8–23).

Some of you need staying power. Times are tough, and you're not sure how long you can last. You're experiencing a significant amount of pain and discomfort. Everything in your gut tells you to run, but if you do, you know it will result in your own emotional and spiritual undoing. You know that sneaking out early will result in others having to cover the bill. It's clear that running may be easiest in the short term, but you can only run for so long and so fast before the same problems catch up with you in a new form. It'd be easy to walk out on a marriage that has lost its flame, to bail on a promise that has become more costly than anticipated, or to take a new job offer and leave a colossal mess in your wake.

You are tired, and the problems surrounding you are starting to close in. Before you go, will you pray and ask God to open your eyes to see the spiritual support surrounding you, the arms that are willing to hold you up? Consider the possibility of staying for the sake of your own personal growth and the salvaging of a relationship. Imagine finding the energy to heal and repair what has been broken. What if instead of burning a bridge, you built an alliance of mutual support?[2]

If comfort is our chief aim in life, we'll look for the quickest way out of the pain and discomfort of the trials we find ourselves in. If we value the inner strength of character above personal comfort, we'll look for opportunities that hide inside the trials we face. Trials endured result in greater perseverance and a more valiant character. Surviving trials develops hope and courage to face the overwhelming obstacles in life and to finally find victory in areas that seem impossible to navigate.

———

The last example of biblical imagery I'll mention involves a lion in a pit on a snowy day and a guy named Benaiah, who jumped into the pit and killed the lion. Well, actually that's the whole story. It feels kind of like a footnote on a list in the Bible. The whole story is told

---

2. "Staying power" does not apply to those in abusive or immoral situations. If you're in a situation like that, please seek help. Professional therapists, easily accessible hotlines, and qualified pastors can help you evaluate your circumstances and identify your options for moving forward.

in one sentence, which comprises just fifteen words and occupies half a verse in the Bible (1 Chronicles 11:22). Benaiah is included on the list of thirty mighty men who valiantly fought to protect David, the king of Israel. He came across a lion in a pit on a snowy day and got down into the pit and killed the lion so the lion wouldn't devour people in the community.

This short story is overflowing with imagery. A lion, in addition to being a real fear-inducing and threatening beast, is a biblical allusion to our ultimate spiritual enemy, Satan, who is said to prowl around like a roaring lion looking to devour God's children (1 Peter 5:8). Benaiah's willingness to get into the pit for the sake of the community is a symbolic foreshadowing of Jesus' courageous action of going down into the pit of the grave to battle death itself, in which his victory affords us rescue from being devoured in the pit of death.

On a practical level, on a daily basis, the lion represents whatever overpowering foe we must face in life. The setting represents our foe appearing at the worst possible time, in the worst possible place—when all the cards are stacked against us. The story concludes with Benaiah's victory, and it's meant to inspire us to be strong and courageous.

What do you most dread? Financial ruin, cancer, estranged children, the exposing of your secret, some life-and-death crisis? What if you had to face that fear—at the worst possible place, at the worst possible time—with every reason to believe you had no chance of victory? Would you walk by the pit in which your foe is temporarily trapped and hope that your enemy won't stalk you later and overtake you and those you love? Or, like Benaiah, would you jump in and fight for the sake of your loved ones?

I want you to hear this. If Benaiah can do it, you can do it. If I can do it, which I did (I'll spend the rest of the book telling you about it), you can do it too. Not because you are a superhero. No illusions of grandeur here. You can jump in, fight for your life, and be victorious, not because you are so impressive, but because God is faithful. He makes the weak formidable. When you grasp that and trust that, you will be surprised at how capable you are. You can be scared yet strong.

FOR REFLECTION

Giving up hurts more than fighting.

---

1. If you made the decision to throw in the towel on a hardship you currently face, what might the consequences be? Remember, not wanting to appear weak is itself a weakness.

2. When was the last time you had to admit to yourself, *I am weak*, in an important area of life? What did it feel like?

CHAPTER 3

Completely Exposed

*I am ready to face any challenges that
might be foolish enough to face me.*

DWIGHT SCHRUTE, *THE OFFICE*

The night before the surgery, I was away from my
home in Orange County, sitting in the backyard of a rented house
in San Francisco surrounded by my family. It was Labor Day 2017,
and we were eating pizza and drinking beer. There was plenty of
that strange kind of conversation that occurs when people just don't
know what to say. Finally, we got on the topic of MRI scans. That
night, I learned that apparently Chuck Norris's wife was poisoned by
the dye injected into her veins during her MRI scans. *Thanks for that.*

I had just completed two days of intense testing, scans, and
brain mapping. I was about to go into brain surgery while remaining conscious. Being awake during surgery would enable me to lie
on the table and ponder if something might go wrong. While a surgeon would remove pieces of my brain, I'd be awake and could worry
about whether I was going to have a stroke or become paralyzed.
At the same time he would be amputating part of my brain, I could
consider that I might lose my mind. I had plenty to be anxious about.

What was completely unexpected was that I was not feeling anxious at all. Instead, I was enjoying my time with Natalie, Hero, and those closest to me and was able to be gracious when people made awkward conversation because they themselves were scared and had no idea what to say to me. After a couple slices of pizza and a beer, I decided to go to bed because I had an early morning the next day. I was tired from all the medical testing I had been through and the endless forms I had filled out. Have you ever been so tired you can't fall asleep? Me too. It happens to me often, and it is infuriating. Typically, I am bad at sleeping. But the night before my surgery, I fell asleep quickly and slept like a baby. When my alarm woke me up the next morning, I felt optimistic and ready to do this thing.

I got out of bed, got dressed, and headed to the hospital with my family. My mood was light, my spirits high. I wasn't giddy, but I was steady. On arrival, they took Natalie and me back to the pre-op area, where we met with Dr. Berger. I was in a hospital-issued gown and fuzzy yellow socks, with Styrofoam dots stuck all over my shaved head that would serve as guides during surgery.

Dr. Berger was already in the zone and definitely had his game face on. He and his crew got me ready and then allowed another person to join me—my pastor, Matthew. We all joked together. The laughter wasn't nervous; it was lighthearted and hopeful. Matthew put a hand on my shoulder and lifted me up in prayer. After he said "Amen," I kissed Natalie goodbye and they wheeled me away on the gurney to the operating room.

Calm in the Storm

The strange thing was the peace.

Even with the circumstances of my life completely out of control, I was experiencing *peace*. Ever since I had made the decision to follow Dr. Berger's recommendation and endure brain surgery while awake, I had been covered by an unmistakable stillness. At the core of my being, I was *calm*. This strikes me as strange because I do not have nerves of steel. I can often be an anxious person, losing sleep as I dwell on worries about the future. The peace was not of me. It was beyond me. It did not come by any therapeutic methods or meditation apps on my phone. The peace came by prayer. It was supernatural, a gracious gift from my heavenly Father to his son who was facing the scariest moment of his life.

I am a man of prayer. Ever since I placed my faith in Jesus as an angry teen who was spinning out of control, prayer has been my anchor. It's often the only thing that can center me and keep me grounded. Interestingly enough, during this whole journey I was not able to pray as often as I normally do. I was experiencing multiple seizures a day, which made it difficult to concentrate and pray. In the course of a month, I had more than one hundred seizures and prayed less often than I ever had in life. I was still able to find peace through prayer by reaching out to others to pray on my behalf. My family, my friends, and my church family all rallied around me in prayer. I went to the elders of my church and asked them for prayer. They surrounded me, laid their hands on my shoulders, anointed me with oil, and prayed bold prayers for healing. And it brought me courage and hope; ultimately, it brought me peace.

I celebrate the fact that this peace wasn't the result of something I was able to do. It feels so gracious and loving to have received this gift despite my own lack of prayer. I was experiencing a frightening storm in my life, but my soul was calm. The experience reminded me of the time when Jesus was on the Sea of Galilee with his disciples in a small, unstable fishing boat and a storm came up. The waves crashed over the boat, and everyone was flung around by tumultuous water, and everyone feared for their lives . . . until Jesus "got up, rebuked the wind and said to the waves, *'Quiet! Be still!'* Then the wind died down and it was completely calm" (Mark 4:39, emphasis added). This is what happened to me. The Spirit of Jesus commanded my soul, "Quiet! Be still!" And it was. It was completely calm.

Even today, Jesus has the power to intervene in the trials, and he is willing to act on behalf of those who journey with him. If you are facing a storm in your life right now and are being tossed around and are barely holding on, terrified of what's going to happen next, you can find peace through prayer. You can pray a very simple but powerful prayer. Ask Jesus to command your soul to be still. Ask Jesus to give you peace.

Awake to Tell about It

The surgical team took me back to the operating room, where the anesthesiologist began the process of putting me to sleep so Dr. Berger could get into my head before waking me up. I didn't know what was waiting for me on the other side of surgery. There were no guarantees. Natalie watched me being wheeled off and was left to wait and wonder if I would make it out of surgery alive. Would that be our last kiss, the last time we'd say we loved each other? She had to sit in a waiting room and wonder if after surgery I'd be the same man she married sixteen years ago.

I knew it was quite possible that the quality of my life would be greatly diminished after surgery. My life span might be shortened significantly. It was likely that after the surgery had ended, some of the tumor would remain and I'd have four years or less of my life to live. My neurosurgeon couldn't make any promises.

But my God has promised me many times that he would never leave me nor forsake me (see Deuteronomy 31:6, 8; Joshua 1:5; 1 Chronicles 28:20; Psalm 94:14; John 14:18; Hebrews 13:5). With God by my side, I could face whatever was waiting for me in the future. That perspective brought me great confidence and peace—which I was going to need because things were about to get crazy.

I quietly slipped into unconsciousness. I was completely unaware as Dr. Berger secured my head in a vice and made a long, elegant incision in my scalp. He folded my face forward and removed a piece of my skull like he was making a jack-o'-lantern at Halloween. Once he was done sawing my skull with a surgical-grade jigsaw and everything was set, they woke me up.

The first thing I remembered when I woke up was a bolt of searing pain, like I had been scalped by a tomahawk. I yelled out in pain. I heard the neurosurgeon say in a calm voice, "Lidocaine." And just like that the pain went away as the cool liquid of the localized anesthetic washed over my scalp. However, the adrenaline from the pain snapped me right out of that dreamlike state that the doctor promised me. I was wide awake. *Wide awake.* My first thought: *My surgeon is a liar! No pain, he said. Dreamlike state, he said.* My second thought: *This is so cool! How many people get to experience this?*

I was not just awake for my surgery; I was *wide awake.* I was completely aware, able to take in every detail and store it in my long-term memory. I wasn't panicked. I wasn't even scared; I was excited. Being fully present for my surgery with an elite surgeon felt like being chosen to ride along with heroic astronauts into space. Although photography wasn't allowed, I took a lot of mental pictures.

Everything was crystal clear. The surgical lights were bright and pure, and they illuminated with hyperreality a surgical team that was monitoring me with hypervigilance. The team was busy checking my vitals, monitoring technology that was mapping my brain in real time, watching my pupils, moving all over the room, communicating with one another. I saw the image of my brain on a monitor, and I thought, *Wow, there's my brain. I can see my brain!*

Then my neurosurgeon, unseen to me, behind me, over me, spoke directly to me: "Jay, how are you?"

"I'm okay," I responded.

He informed me, "I'm going to push on different parts of your brain with an electrode, and I need you to tell me where you feel it in your body, okay?"

"Okay."

He pushed the electrode onto my brain, and I could feel my left arm tighten up.

I reported to him, "Left arm."

"Good," he said. He pushed again, and I felt my left leg jolt.

I reported, "Left leg."

Then he asked, "Can you feel this in your mouth?" As he pushed down, I felt an illusion of my tongue expanding in my mouth, swelling, plumping, growing.

"Yuurph, muy toooongh pheeelz phat."

And on and on it went, Dr. Berger querying my cognitive ability and watching that my limbs didn't jerk unexpectedly. He was confirming that the preoperative brain mapping was accurate so he could have a pretty good feel for the way the removal of each slice of brain tissue might affect me permanently.

"Scissors," I heard him say. Then I heard a noise that was louder than Dr. Berger's voice. *SNIP. SNIP. SNIP.* My open cranium became a concert hall, with acoustical reverberations of each cut. I could hear the workings of each tool with amplification. *Snips, slices, spinning, drilling.* No pain, just sounds. I was fully aware that the surgeon was removing portions of my brain. I could tell he was working on the outer region of my brain for an hour and a half or so. Then I could tell he made his move and was burrowing into the inner cortex. *This is it*, I thought. *This is what matters. This is what determines success or failure. This is the danger zone.*

My thoughts were as sharp as the surgeon's tools. I was aware of the risk, but I was not afraid. I was completely out of control, my life in the hands of a surgeon as he navigated past a major artery and began to remove portions of brain that potentially contribute to making me . . . me. I needed him to keep me safe. I needed him to push as far as possible, remove as much of the tumor as possible, extend my life as long as possible. And I was praying for God's hands to guide the surgeon's hand. I was praying for God to perform a miracle and remove the entire tumor, despite Dr. Berger's research that predicted otherwise.

It still amazes me today that I was not nervous at that moment. I was completely exposed and vulnerable, yet calm, quiet, and at peace. People were praying for me every minute of my surgery. Some were fasting on my behalf. A high school teacher had her choir singing songs of praise over me. I was held at peace by the presence of God through it all.

Natalie sat in the waiting room with the family and friends who had made the trip out to San Francisco. She had recently sat in the waiting room while her mom was having surgery to remove tumors from her gastrointestinal tract. Exhausted from the difficult experience of her mom's surgery, she was facing an intense time of waiting once again. Hero was sick and stayed back at the house with a babysitter. Natalie was separated from us both for hours. She was tired and stressed but also very hopeful. She went for walks, prayed, received updates, and waited.

After two and a half hours of being awake as a portion of my brain was strategically removed, I was exhausted. The surgeon said, "Okay, that's all we need from you. Let's put you back to sleep." As I slipped back into unconsciousness, I could only hope that they had gotten it all. *Please, God*, I prayed, *help them get it all.* I needed the entire tumor to be removed. Any remaining tumor would poison me and encroach for a few years before overtaking my brain and taking my life.

Back to sleep I went.

When I was twenty-six years old—a decade before my brain tumor troubles—I learned about the fragility of life. My dad was one year away from retirement when suddenly, out of nowhere, he suffered a heart attack, was rushed to the hospital, and pulled through. My sister went directly to the hospital and sat with him as he recovered. I was an hour away, with no idea of what had happened.

My sister and my dad talked for thirty minutes. He was focused on the big questions of life and expressed a desire to make his life matter. Then my sister left to pick up her son from school. Moments after she left the room, my dad had another heart attack and died. My sister called me at work and told me. I was stunned, with absolutely no idea of how to react. I got in my car and drove to my parents' house, where I comforted my mom and connected with my sister. When Natalie showed up, we went into the guest bedroom, crumbled onto the bed, and wept bitterly. The dominating thought in my mind and heart was this: *death is terrible, and my faith is not bringing me comfort the way I thought it would.*

My sadness was quickly engulfed in anger. I had heard many times before, and had even affirmed myself, that God is big enough to handle our anger—we don't need to hold back from him. So I vented my anger on him. *Why would you take my dad before allowing him to enjoy his retirement?* My dad had so many interesting plans. He was the safety net for our family. Why would God take him prematurely and leave us to flounder without him? I prayed with raw honesty, expecting that venting my anger would bring relief. Instead, I was growing angrier. I was becoming reckless in my personal life and found solace in riding my motorcycle way too fast. I was taking unnecessary risks.

As my anger grew, I also grew uneasy at work. It's hard for a pastor to teach every weekend about the goodness of God while also being pissed off at God. The dissonance was too much to cope with. I needed resolution with God. I turned to the method that has been most effective when I desperately need to hear from God—fasting in the wilderness. I packed a small tent, a light sleeping bag, an axe, matches, and water. I told Natalie I would be gone for a couple days, and I headed to Mammoth Mountain.

After driving five hours north of Orange County, I got a camping spot in a park-and-pitch site where I slept the first night. Early the next morning, I headed into the woods. I hiked all day and tried to pray. My mind wandered. I couldn't focus or connect with God—nor could I as the sun set and I sat by the fire I had made. I went to bed that evening hungry and discouraged. The next morning, I woke up even hungrier and still feeling distant from God. I spent another day and night hiking and trying to pray, but to no avail. When I woke up the next morning, even angrier at God, I decided to hike back, make breakfast, and declare my journey to be over, conceding defeat.

I drove home very confused. Before this point, whenever I sought the Lord, I found him. When I called out to him, in one way or another he answered. But not this time. All I heard was silence, and all I felt was distance—and frustration. I wondered if the death of my father would also be the death of my faith.

And then the next song on my playlist came on, and something broke. The song began quietly—a folk song perfect for driving a long stretch through the wilderness. Then the chorus hit, and the mood of the song suddenly changed: "So f*** you, f*** you, f*** you and all we've been through."[1] I screamed along at the top of my lungs. I screamed the lyrics in God's face, and it was as if God finally heard me. I cursed God, and he responded with unmerited grace. He answered me with revelation and insight in my soul. I was reminded of what I already knew but had lost sight of. The Lord ministered to my spirit. God spoke:

> *You are right, Jay, death is terrible. You have experienced the pain of losing your dad, and I have experienced the pain of losing my Son, Jesus. I hated death in that moment, as I always have and as I hate it now. I hate watching my dearly loved child hurt so badly—I am not apathetic. I have not stood back and done nothing. I hate death even more than*

---

1. Damien Rice, "Rootless Tree," track 4 on *9*, Warner Bros., 2006.

you do—so much so that I have battled death head-on and by the power of love have overcome it. All who trust in me will overcome it too. There is a time when I will set all things right, but I am patiently waiting and must ask my children to endure the pain of loss, though it is only temporary.

And with those wise words whispered to my soul, my misplaced anger found its rightful landing place—*death itself is my enemy.*

———

It felt like only seconds before I was awake again after the surgery. The first thing I remember is Natalie. It was just she and I. I don't remember the room, the bed, or the bandage. She remembers each of those details with vivid quality. I just remember her presence. It was comforting, warm, and safe. Her face was beautiful, her voice soothing as she said her first words to me: "They got it all." She was an angel announcing a miracle. Relief, victory, joy, life washed over me. "They got it all," she said again.

Then pure joy entered the room. Hero ran in smiling and calling my name: "Daddy!" She climbed into bed with me. I held her in my arms and thanked God that I could be there for her—to hold her when she was hurt, teach her how to drive, walk her down the aisle, maybe even hold her child in my arms.

I knew instantly I had been the recipient of a miracle. Over the course of the next year, many other surgeons and specialists confirmed how unlikely it had been for me to have such a perfect outcome. No residual tumor, no cognitive or psychological impairment. Natalie was continually surprised at how such important portions of my brain were removed with no damage to my daily functioning. My hair grew back, and the scar wasn't even visible. I felt like my surgical story mirrored the biblical story of Shadrach, Meshach, and Abednego, who were given a death sentence, thrown into a fiery furnace, and rescued by God. When they walked out of the flames, "there was no smell of fire on them" (Daniel 3:27)!

Dr. Berger is an exceptional surgeon, but when I saw the absolute awe on the faces of the other surgeons when they reviewed my postoperative scans, I knew this was beyond what any man could perform on his own. I credit Dr. Berger for the first 80 percent; I credit God for the "impossible" remaining 20 percent. I truly believe that the hand of God miraculously guided the neurosurgeon's hand that day.

Spiritual Strength Is Steady in the Storm

My all-time favorite verse in the Bible is found in an obscure book written by a minor prophet named Zephaniah:

> The LORD your God is with you,
>   the Mighty Warrior who saves.
> He will take great delight in you . . .
>   [and] will rejoice over you with singing.
> **(ZEPHANIAH 3:17)**

When I first read this verse, I was shocked. I could hardly believe it. I was a brand-new Christian who didn't know much. What I did know was that Christians got together every Sunday to sing praise music about Jesus. When I sang these songs, I felt such love and delight in Jesus.

Before becoming a Christian, I had never before rejoiced with singing. When I discovered Zephaniah 3:17, I couldn't believe that God felt the same way about me and even returned my joyful singing with his own songs that express his delight in me. But now, I had experienced this truth firsthand. He sang his peace over me before surgery. His battle hymn kept me safe under the knife, and his song concluded with a doctor proclaiming a clean bill of health.

God rejoices over all his children. He sings for us all. I am not privileged or special. He sings over me, and he sings over you. I received a miracle not because of who I am but because of who God is—a Mighty Warrior who saves and delights in us. I don't know exactly how this miracle happened or why I experienced something so rare, but I do know that our God is a healing God. He is a concerned Father. And he is not restricted to the realm above. When he wills, he can reach into our world and touch our lives. He can fix, forgive, and make things right again. We can pray boldly, take steps of faith, and remained centered on the peace that God provides.

Are you facing a seemingly impossible situation? Do you have an unsolvable problem in your life? Are you confronting a crisis over which you have no control? Do you need God to intervene? What miracle do you need? Do you have a health problem that doctors can't figure out? Do you have a condition that currently has no cure? Has your disease progressed beyond hope? Is your family drowning in dysfunction? Are you barely treading water, wondering how much longer you can stay afloat? Have your finances been turned upside down? Has your life's boat been capsized? Has addiction, anger, or anxiety grabbed hold of you and dragged you down? If you are feeling scared, anxious, or hopeless, take heart. Your God can calm the storm and break every chain that holds you in bondage.

Do you need God to show up? He is close at hand. Reach out to him, for he is there. Do you need God's attention? He is all ears. Call out to him in prayer, and he will hear your cry. Do you need God's peace? Take your next step, trusting that he is already with you. Make your decision, and let the peace of God fill your soul. Pray! Let the power of prayer bring you into the presence of God.

Listen to what God is saying to you:

"When you call on me, when you come and pray to me, I'll listen."
(JEREMIAH 29:12 MSG)

"Therefore I tell you, whatever you ask for in prayer, believe that you have received it, and it will be yours." **(MARK 11:24)**

Be joyful in hope, patient in affliction, faithful in prayer. **(ROMANS 12:12)**

Never will I leave you; never will I forsake you. **(HEBREWS 13:5)**

Be strong and courageous, knowing that if God is for you, there is nothing to fear. He has the power to move mountains or he will lend you his strength to climb the mountain before you. His strength is unending. The key to having the strength to face tomorrow is having the faith that God is with you today, sustaining you with his grace.

Pray to your God. When you are unable to pray, ask others to pray on your behalf. When you feel distant from him, seek him. Drive to the desert. Fast. Question him. Wrestle with him. Scream at him. Call out to him. And when he answers, rejoice in him. Remember that he rejoices in you. Do not expect him to act according to some formula. That's not how he works. But do trust his nature. He mysteriously acts according to his unchanging character.

You can trust who God is, even when the way forward is confusing. Often you won't know what circumstances are waiting for you on the other side of the chasm of crisis that you face. But with certainty you can know that God is waiting on the other side and will walk with you on your next step. With God by your side, you can face anything. God provides spiritual strength that keeps you steady in the storm.

I believe that miracles still happen today. My miracle is temporary. I may have escaped an incurable tumor by way of a miraculous surgery, but my life will end one day, just like everyone else's. But through faith in Jesus, I know I have eternal life. Though my life will end here on earth, I will step into true and eternal life. My medical miracle was not guaranteed, but the miracle of eternal life *is* guaranteed. It is the greatest miracle possible, and it is guaranteed by Jesus to all who place their faith in him:

> "I can guarantee this truth: Those who listen to what I say and believe in the one who sent me will have eternal life." (JOHN 5:24 GW)

If you are unsure of where you stand with God, undecided on what you believe about Jesus—if you have been investigating God and have felt him pursuing you but something has been holding you back, something has kept you from taking that step of faith—will you allow my story to give you the courage to trust Jesus and to dedicate your life to God? If you turn to God, he will welcome you with open arms. If you confess your sin, he will forgive you. If you dedicate your life to him, he will give you eternal life. God can be trusted. For the Bible says, "Anyone who believes in him will never be put to shame" (Romans 10:11).

If you have trusted God with your life, both immediately and eternally, will you allow him to write the story he wills for you—even if the path is terrifying? When he leads you through deep waters and the waves of life threaten to overwhelm you, will you cry out to Jesus to calm the storm in your soul? Spiritual strength is steady in the storm because the Spirit of God is with you. In God's presence is courage. He will not forsake you. Give all your worries and cares to God, for he cares about you (1 Peter 5:7).

So cast your anxiety on God and take on his strength and courage in your soul. Stay strong and press on, steady in the storm.

You are given one life. Live it well. I want to live a life of faith and love, focusing on eternal things and staying connected to Jesus, the ultimate giver of life. Nothing else matters.

_____

*When you are unaware of the divine help and
supernatural strength that is available to you, you
may find yourself running from a fight you can win.*

_____

1. In what area of your life does fear have a foothold? If fear weren't present, what is the first thing you would do?

2. Above all else, what truly matters to you? Write out some specifics about the legacy you hope to leave.

CHAPTER 4

The Greater Miracle

You get what you want, but not what you need.

COLDPLAY, "FIX YOU"

Surviving an incurable brain tumor through the hand of God is not the only miracle I have received. The second, greater miracle was not something God did *for* me, but rather something God did *in* me. God not only restored my life; he also orchestrated an inner healing that is waking me up and allowing me to become fully alive. I am starting to experience life to the full, just as Jesus intended.

My life began with the odds stacked against me. From the very beginning, the stage was set for a miracle to be performed in my heart. I was born into a chaotic family system. My mom, who struggled with mental health issues and whose self-medication attempts had led to substance abuse issues, also struggled with postpartum depression after I was born. She tried to care for me, her newborn son, but her depression crippled her, causing her to neglect me for a long period of time when I was just an infant. My mom was unable to handle the demands of a totally dependent second baby while caring for a toddler daughter. All she could bring herself to do for a time was to get out of bed and sit in the backyard, staring out into the distance, leaving her kids to fend for themselves.

Of course, I don't have actual memories of the first two years of my life when I experienced neglect, but I do have the memory of being an adult and having my mom confess this to me. She spoke of it in a matter-of-fact manner, but I saw shame in her eyes. Her voice was trying to dismiss the levity of her deficiencies in my early life, but her eyes betrayed her and let me see her deep regret. When she told me of her neglect, she and I both knew it was worthy of sadness, but neither of us knew how deeply wounding those years were for me. It wasn't until I was married with a baby daughter of my own that I began to understand the impact of my early childhood.

As my mom sat in the backyard on her chair, I was hard at work developing my little brain. As my synapses were forming, I was developing an understanding that I was on my own. Beyond a cognitive thought, I had intuitive knowledge that the person I was supposed to be able to count on was not dependable. This forged in me a resilience and independence that served me well. It helped me survive a threatening childhood and thrive in school and later in my career. I am a highly motivated self-starter. In group situations, I take the lead. When obstacles to success arise, I persevere, even when others on my team give up. I get it done. You don't need to pay me more money. Just allow me autonomy, a sense of ownership, and clear markers of success that are challenging yet realistically obtainable, and I will be content to work my hardest. I am not exceptionally intelligent, but my grade point average in high school was above a 4.0, and I tested in the ninety-ninth percentile for reasoning. While defending my master's thesis, my judging panel recommended me to pursue PhD candidacy. At work I am consistently identified as a top performer. My resiliency and independence made me a great student and employee. However, it did not put me in a position to be a great husband or father.

Don't get me wrong, I'm a stand-up guy by all outward

appearances. I am not a deadbeat dad or terrible husband. But there are limitations that no one can see other than myself, my wife, and, to a certain extent, my daughter. I have tried to confide in close friends about my resistance to connect with Natalie and Hero, but they couldn't see what I was trying to describe. Instead, they'd conclude I was being hard on myself and told me I was experiencing the normal difficulties of marriage and parenting. But I knew there was something deeper. Something was blocking me from connecting at a deeper level. I was performing the mechanics of marriage and parenting at a somewhat satisfactory level . . . maybe a solid C-. But the level of true connection was lacking. I simultaneously desired a deep connection with loved ones and feared what it might reveal to those I was trying to connect with.

I've known for a long time that I lack the ability to connect deeply with the ones I love the most. There have been times when I have desperately wanted to connect with my loved ones authentically and openly, and there's an equal number of times I'm too afraid to reach out for fear of being let down by the ones I expected to be there for me. An even greater fear than being let down is being discovered to be weak. What if I relied on someone to be there for me and they inevitably bailed on me, what if they saw the panic in my eyes and knew how weak and dependent I am? To some, it'd be no big deal. To me, it was everything. There is nothing more pathetic to me than being clingy and needy. Feeling weak seems pathetic.

To let someone in and allow them to know the depths of my soul would be to allow them to see my weakness, which I hide even from myself. But to continue to limit my vulnerability would perpetuate a lack of meaningful connection in my life. So my fear of weakness is my greatest weakness.

My reflections here may seem quite abstract. Here's an example of how being fearful and connection-averse plays out in my life. Natalie offered to go to every one of my medical appointments with me leading up to the surgery. I told her it wasn't necessary. I didn't want her to have to miss work. She had Hero to worry about, who was only four years old at the time, and I didn't need her to worry about me. I didn't want to inconvenience her or put unnecessary stress on her, even though I knew she wanted to be there with me.

I had witnessed her drive four hours one way, from Southern California to Central California, to attend medical appointments with her mom, who had been fighting cancer for years. She once drove a friend two hours to a consultation with a therapist she recommended. She never complained about these things. Natalie is truly a kind and caring person. She values being available for friends in need and finds purpose in serving her loved ones as they walk through trials in life. Yet she isn't pushy. And so she simply offered to go with me to my appointments and backed off when I dismissed her offer to help.

When I essentially said, "Thanks, but no thanks," I really thought I was being loving toward Natalie. I thought I was being a noble guy by not burdening my wife. I assumed that Natalie received my response as I intended. It wasn't until after my brain surgery that I learned I was wrong. My refusal of her help caused Natalie pain, made her feel distant from me, and left her confused.

Shortly after I refused Natalie's offer, my friend Kevin, who earlier in my story made sure I wasn't mistreated by a difficult-to-navigate health care system and who sometimes has a brazen and intrusive personality, learned that I was going to appointments alone. "Don't you ever go to an appointment alone," Kevin lectured. "I will take you to every single one. If you get bad news, you shouldn't be driving. I don't care what day or time your appointment is, call me and I'll drop everything to be there. Just don't go alone."

I obeyed. Every time I had an appointment scheduled, I called Kevin. Faithful to his word, he took me every time, except for the one time I snuck out on my own. Kevin went out of his way for me, and as a result we bonded. I will always remember him as the guy who was there for me. If I get in a pinch again, I believe that Kevin will insist on being with me. On one car ride, he told me, "We are brothers forever. You can't get rid of me." I agreed.

Issues of the Heart

Seeing Kevin accompany me to appointments must have been awful for Natalie. To offer to be there for me, only to have me reject her help and accept the same offer from another person, must have deeply hurt Natalie and confused her—a sort of confusion she had grown accustomed to by virtue of being married to me. *Why does he do that?* she must have asked a million different times in a million similar but different situations. It was a question I never even thought to ask myself. I was completely blind to this tendency in myself. But ever since experiencing what it's like to be completely vulnerable during surgery, I have woken up and am learning to see things differently. I am conscious to parts of me I was never aware of before. I am now finding the courage to view myself with the integrity of reality.

Why did I refuse help from my wife but not my friend? I have learned that I am good at allowing people to do things for me, but I am terrible at allowing people to be there for me. In principle, it is hard to distinguish one from another. In reality, there's a big difference. Getting a ride to my appointment is a task; going with someone to an appointment is a connection. I could jump into Kevin's car, give him an update on the progress of my journey, and never mention an emotion beyond the word *frustration*. He would comment on things he sensed I was feeling, but I wouldn't engage him on that topic for long. I didn't want him to see me struggle because I didn't want him to see me as weak. I'd let him do things for me, but I wouldn't let him in.

If I would have let Natalie go with me to my appointments, I couldn't have avoided talking about emotions. Although she is not intrusive, she is intuitive, and I cannot hide my feelings from her.

Even if I tried to look strong, she would see my frail reality. As my wife, she would have appropriately asked probing questions and pressed me on issues of the heart.

I had one appointment I intentionally went to alone. It was the type of appointment that had potential for really bad news to be shared about my expected length of life. No one knew the nature of the appointment other than me. I went alone and planned some margin in my schedule so that I'd have time afterward to sit on the beach and process. I even planned to go by Natalie's favorite bakery and bring her back a surprise in order for the isolation to seem valiant.

What I was really doing, though unknowingly at that point, was buying myself time in case I had to process bad information, confront my weakness, and compose myself before seeing anyone so no one would see me as I really was—namely, weak. The appointment didn't hold any worse news than I had already received, but my fear had isolated me even further than I had already been. I was fearful of connection, and so I avoided connecting too deeply. My fear made me detached. And being detached left me with a sense of dissatisfaction, which I kind of liked and kind of hated.

I have spent a considerable amount of time in prayer, requesting God's help in this dilemma. I've also spent much time and energy in therapy. I worked well with therapists. I gravitated toward those who implemented cognitive behavioral techniques, and I always completed the homework they gave me. Whatever they suggested, I tried. I've had times in my life when I've resolved to trust God, embrace my weakness, and connect with others. At times I've dedicated all my willpower to overcoming my limitations of connectivity. However, I've never had enough inner resolve to make significant progress.

At times I try to create work-arounds to manage my shortcomings. I've read books on attachment theory that suggest the hardwiring my brain experienced during the time of neglect at a young age made lasting imprints on all my current and future attachment relationships. I've wondered if I would ever genuinely want to connect deeply with loved ones. I thought perhaps I could find tools to help keep me from distancing myself too far from others, even if I never actually wanted to come too close.

At any rate, my problem didn't seem to have a solution. I was at a loss. I retreated and settled in to anticipate a dissatisfying life of disconnection for which there was no cure—that is, until I faced a life-threatening illness and a highly uncertain surgery, which began to press in on me until finally something broke free. Suddenly I now desire deep, meaningful connection. Another miracle. A greater miracle!

As my surgery approached, God was working to heal not only my brain but also my heart. Although I had declined to allow my wife to go to my preoperative appointments, God had impressed wisdom on my heart: *You are going to need your wife if you are going to face this, and you are going to need your daughter if you are going to get past this.* So in a very unfair way, I told Natalie I needed her to be available to me. I will keep the details of the conversation private, but essentially I allowed my fear to blame her for not being available to me in the past. It goes without saying that the conversation didn't go well, and yet Natalie gracefully agreed to do whatever I needed in order to be available for me.

Once we arrived in San Francisco to the home where we'd stay during the days leading up to the surgery and the week afterward, I asked if I could have the room with the window that looked out onto the back patio so I could watch Hero play. Although I didn't verbalize it, I wanted to see my daughter, full of joy and life, playing in the backyard as a source of motivation for my healing and a source of joy in the midst of pain, in case of any major complications in the surgery that might result in a difficult recovery.

In the previous chapter, I mentioned that when I woke up from the surgery, my beautiful wife was the first thing I saw. Natalie's soothing voice was the first thing I heard, angelically proclaiming the miracle of God. When I retell the story, this is always the part at which I tear up. Most people assume my emotion is the result of experiencing God's miracle and regaining my life. Yes, that's a big part of it, of course, but the truth is, some of the most intense emotion comes from the connection I felt with Natalie in that moment. I had never been weaker or more vulnerable, and I had never been happier to see her. Despite my tendency to recoil in those moments, I loved the feeling of connection. The remarkable thing is that it was not a momentary experience; the desire to remain connected has stuck with me. This is a new normal in my life. The shackles of my heart have been unfastened. I feel truly free.

In an instant, I was changed. My desire for closeness to my wife and daughter was tangible. This is new, uncharted territory for me, but it is totally within my reach to learn how to navigate these connected waters. Currently, I'm clumsy in my connection attempts and can be a bit unrealistic in what I expect in return. But in time, I will learn how to live a deeply connected life. It was the *desire* I couldn't manufacture, but God changed that for me.

I've only begun to scratch the surface of what has happened to me since my surgery. A friend and a fellow pastor, Pete Shambrook, has told me that what took place can be seen as a progressive revelation. He described the moment when I came out of brain surgery as a *new birth*. When I was born, I opened my eyes to a world in which I couldn't rely on my mom—my primary attachment figure—to be there for me. Because of my lack of attachment, I became more vulnerable to stress, lack of emotional regulation, and an inability to trust.

Out of fear, I kept everyone at arm's length, especially those closest to me. Both of my parents have now passed away and I've started a new family. When I opened my eyes after surgery, Natalie and Hero were there for me. It took a traumatic event in which I was fully exposed and completely weak and vulnerable to truly understand that I was no longer on my own but had people I could trust. The people closest to me were reliable.

In no way could I have manufactured this scenario. Processing through my trauma in a therapist's office wasn't enough. It was only the hand of God, taking a terrifying incident and working good from it, that could get through to my heavily guarded heart.

It was miraculous that God saved my life from an encroaching, unstoppable tumor. To me, it's an even greater miracle that he saved me from living the rest of my life only half alive. I am now free and on the path to love and be fully loved, to know and be fully known. I have dedicated the next years of my life to learning how to live a connected kind of life. If God hadn't miraculously healed me, I figure I would have wanted to live my last years with great purpose. But I was saved from death, this time, but I know I *will* die at some point. So I should still use the years I have been given to live fully alive and fully connected with my loved ones.

I was saved from a disconnected life, and the connections I forge in my relationships in this life will endure for eternity. For this miracle of being able to desire this kind of deep connection I am forever grateful. Praise be to God!

God's Strength Breaks Chains

Trust in the Lord with your whole heart and don't lean on your own understanding (Proverbs 3:5) because God's way is perfect (2 Samuel 22:31) and God's foolishness is wiser than human wisdom, and his weakness stronger than human strength (1 Corinthians 1:25). You know what you want and you think you know what you need. Pray and tell God the desires of your heart. If your desires and requests are good, he will give them to you. And thankfully, God "is able to do immeasurably more than all we ask or imagine, according to his power that is at work within us, to him be glory" (Ephesians 3:20–21).

Try something new. Pray differently. When you ask God for

something specific, end by saying, "Surprise me." Who knows, you might get what you want and more. Or you might avoid getting what you asked for—something that might have worked against you—and be given something better instead. Before you ask, visualize yourself in church singing praises to God. Then visualize him singing back over you, delighted that you are his child. Then ask for what you need, as a child asks their father, who is a great gift giver. Be patient, waiting on the Lord with expectancy, and give him freedom to work. Don't just ask him to work miracles *for* you; ask him to work miracles *in* you. See if this approach revolutionizes not only your prayer life but also your relationship with God.

I still have a chasm to cross when it comes to vulnerability. I am learning and I am becoming. Here is a truth I can pass on to you: Vulnerability is not weakness. Vulnerability takes strength. Vulnerability *is* strength.

I've always tried to live life to the fullest. I've run with the bulls in Spain. Natalie and I went skydiving on our honeymoon. In college, I used to sneak into places for the thrill of it. I snuck into huge concerts and then made my way backstage. I snuck into a WWE event, went backstage, and got thrown out of the building by an intimidating wrestler named Mankind. I've lived a bucket-list-worthy life. I can tell you there has been nothing scarier than to try to live a vulnerable life. And I can tell you if you want to live fully alive, being vulnerable *must* be a part of the equation. Let's give it a shot.

Life in and of itself is a miracle. I've had the rare experience of witnessing a miracle of healing in my lifetime, which led to a greater miracle of inner healing. I'm seeing firsthand that God is more than able and more than willing to break chains. What a ride life is! Make the most of it.

Like it is with any weakness, becoming stronger in the area of vulnerability is uncomfortable. Here are a few things I'm trying to do to practice getting comfortable with vulnerability:

- → **Add emotion.** Don't just tell your loved ones what happened; include sharing how it made you feel.
- → **Acknowledge embarrassment.** At the end of the day, tell the person you're closest to the one thing that happened that day that most embarrassed you. Take note of how common (and funny) your embarrassing moment is.
- → **Admit the fragility of life.** As a friend once advised me, conduct a near-death experiment. Pick a day to pretend you're going to die tomorrow while also dreaming that you'll live forever, and see how that changes you.

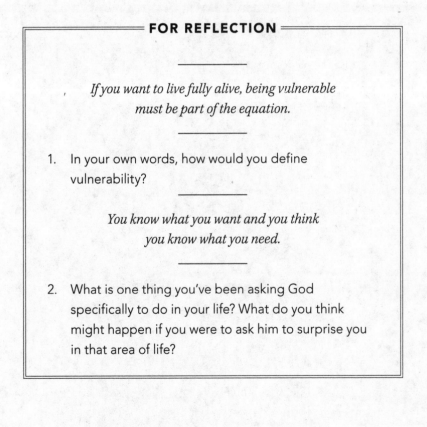

FOR REFLECTION

If you want to live fully alive, being vulnerable must be part of the equation.

1. In your own words, how would you define vulnerability?

You know what you want and you think you know what you need.

2. What is one thing you've been asking God specifically to do in your life? What do you think might happen if you were to ask him to surprise you in that area of life?

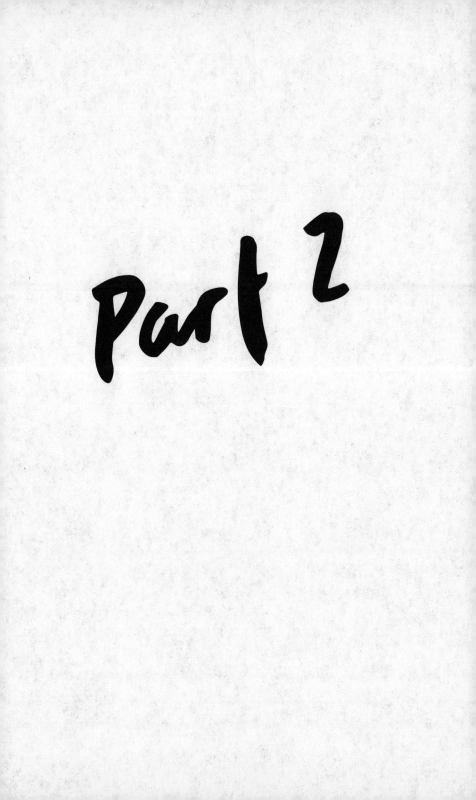

Part 2

CHAPTER 5

The Answer Is No (and That's Okay)

Do I contradict myself?
Very well then, I contradict myself.
(I am large. I contain multitudes.)

WALT WHITMAN

Things are good now, right? I experienced a miracle of healing. God did a work of healing in my life that was both outward and inward. Obviously, God spared my life because he has a special purpose for me, right? I can relax now because my life has been restored, and I've got a good shot at celebrating my eightieth birthday, right?

Wrong.

A year after my miraculously successful surgery and my clean bill of health, I had a seizure. It seemed to come out of nowhere. I had been here before and was shocked to be back again. I went in for an MRI. I prayed, prayed, and prayed some more before the procedure, pleading with God to hear my doctor say, "Your scan looks clean. No sign of a tumor." I prayed that this recent seizure resulted from the surgery, not because of a new tumor. I knew that a new tumor would only equal one thing—*cancer*.

I went to my appointment full of anxiety. My doctor came in and pulled up the scan. "Your tumor has recurred." What he was really saying in those words was simple.

You have terminal brain cancer.

It had been an unintentional setup. Initially my medical team had thought that because they removed my original tumor completely and in time, I was in the clear, with a clean bill of health. But now a new tumor had formed. It was clear from this fact that my brain was filled with cancer cells that weren't detectable by the human eye during surgery or by an MRI scan after surgery. As they explained to me, the cancer cells scattered throughout my brain are in a sense *turned off*—until they aren't. When they eventually turn on, which they will, they come together to form a new tumor. And within a few years, the chances were good that the cancer cells would overtake my brain and end my life.

I was going to need a second brain surgery—a procedure that would be followed by radiation and chemotherapy. They explained very clearly that the radiation and chemotherapy would not destroy the cancer cells but would only *stun* them, hopefully keeping them at bay and slowing down the rate at which they would form new tumors.

Natalie and I sat in the small office of my new neuro-oncologist, Dr. Nancy Bush. With no-holds-barred honesty and kindness in her voice, she told us, "This kind of cancer has no cure. It's terminal." I heard Natalie's quiet tears and turned to her, placing my hand on her knee, trying to offer comfort I knew couldn't be enough. Together we were about to face something we desperately wanted to avoid.

Dr. Bush offered reassurance and said, "There is no cure for this kind of cancer—*yet*. My job is to keep you alive long enough for the medical community to find a cure." Unfortunately, cancer researchers haven't made any significant progress in this area for more than two decades.

The clock was ticking.

What! It made no sense to me. Why would God deliver me from a nearly inoperable tumor through a high-risk surgery with miraculous results, only to have the tumor recur and for me to receive an unfavorable prognosis that essentially amounted to a death sentence? At this point I began to realize I was a brain tumor survivor who was now battling a terminal brain cancer. I was in a fight I could not win.

What would you do if you heard the words "you have cancer" along with the words "no cure" and "terminal"? I'll tell you what I did. I went to Dunkin'. I wanted to drown my sorrows with a maple bar. I used the drive-through, parked in the parking lot, and then got down to business with God.

I prayed, *God, what are you doing?* It wasn't an angry prayer, like when my dad died. It was a confused prayer. It was very straightforward. I asked God, *What are you doing?* and then he answered.

It was not a booming voice from heaven. Instead it was just as Jesus promised. The Holy Spirit unmistakably communicated to me by reminding me of what Jesus had said before. My mind went to 2 Corinthians 12:6–10 (a passage I hadn't yet memorized), and I felt a bond with the apostle Paul. In this passage, Paul was dealing with what he described as "a thorn in my flesh"—a mysterious statement that some scholars believe referred to a medical condition with no treatment.[1] Paul had a *thorn in his flesh*, while I had a *tumor in my brain*.

Paul had asked repeatedly for healing, as had I. The answer Paul received from Jesus was the same one I had received: *No.* But with compassion, Jesus essentially explained to Paul, "My grace is

---

1. In 2 Corinthians 12, Paul didn't explicitly say that the "thorn in my flesh" was a medical issue. Some scholars believe he was referring to an illness, while others believe he was referring to persecution. Either way, he was facing an unsolvable problem that was threatening to bring his ministry to a halt. The undisputed truth of the Scripture is that God is a deliverer and that we can count on him when there seems to be no way forward. I take comfort in this truth.

sufficient, and my power is best displayed in weakness." After hearing this, Paul concluded, "When I am weak, then I am strong." The Holy Spirit ministered to my spirit, and I concluded the same thing: "When I am weak, then I am strong."

I got a strong sense that God was going to use my weakness to teach me the true meaning of strength. And also that this next season of my life would allow me to become vulnerable with my wife and daughter and form a deep connection with them. In that moment, God granted me insight: cancer was not the undoing of the miracle, but rather the *continuation* of the work he had begun.

After I came out of surgery, God miraculously granted me a desire in my heart to connect deeply with my family. But what I didn't know at the time was that I would need more than just a desire to connect. For deep relational connection to occur, I'd need to unlearn the patterns I had developed due to childhood trauma. In order to connect with Natalie and Hero as deeply as my heart now desired, I'd need to learn to be vulnerable and let my weakness show. It would be a long, hard road. I would never have chosen cancer as the pathway to connection, but as I sat with my maple bar and my God, I felt clarity descend on the confusion. God was not negating the earlier miracle and ignoring my prayers. To say yes to one of my prayers, he would need to say no to another prayer. Sometimes God often says no to a prayer in order to say yes to the true desires of our hearts. Deep connection is the desire of my heart that I had been praying for. I truly believe my diagnosis is a key part of my continuing emotional healing that is allowing me to forge deep connection.

Let me be very clear. I do not want to have cancer. I desperately want to be healed from this vicious disease—both emotionally and physically. I am reminded of Jesus' interaction with a man who was paralyzed (Matthew 9:1–8). Hoping for a miracle of physical healing, his friends had taken him to see Jesus teach but weren't able to get into the building. So they climbed onto the roof, lifted their buddy up, and started tearing off the clay roof! Ignoring the complaints of the crowd below, they kept destroying the roof until they made a hole big enough for their friend to fit through. Then they lowered him down and dropped him right in front of Jesus. That's one way to get God's attention!

Jesus stopped teaching, having recognized that the guy was paralyzed, and said to him, "Son, your sins are forgiven." *What!* Jesus' words must have made no sense to the disabled man. He had gone through so much to get to Jesus—the one who had healed so many others whom doctors couldn't help. But instead of attending to his immediate and intense problem, Jesus addressed the man's deeper, more consequential spiritual problem.

After forgiving his sins, Jesus then healed the man's legs and he was able to walk for the first time! Jesus is compassionate enough to heal completely—physically, emotionally, and spiritually. Perhaps Jesus is currently continuing to heal my emotions and attending to the deepest desire of my heart as I fight terminal cancer. Perhaps once the emotional healing is complete he will attend to my physical healing. I can't pretend to know his will or the details of how he works. But I do know I have his attention. I know he cares about me and his will is good. Despite having a hard road to walk, God has given me enough understanding to have peace as I walk. After all, Jesus had to walk a hard road, but he was able to understand the glory awaiting him on the other side of the cross. Same with Paul, who followed in his footsteps. I signed up to follow Jesus. So as I follow in his footsteps I am not surprised that my path is difficult. I'm not surprised and I'm secure knowing he is with me. Same for you. Life is hard, but following Jesus and allowing his Spirit to guide you will allow you to avoid being surprised by suffering and instead stand firm in the security of his presence. When you are able to acknowledge the nearness of Christ in difficulty, you will experience the hope that good things lie ahead. The apostle Peter says it best, "Dear friends, do not be surprised at the fiery ordeal that has come on you to test you, as though something strange were happening to you. But rejoice inasmuch as you participate in the sufferings of Christ, so that you may be overjoyed when his glory is revealed" (1 Peter 4:12–13).

Thorn in the Flesh

I now feel a special bond with the apostle Paul when I read his second letter to the church in Corinth. It's amazing how trauma can bond people. I think Paul and I have both experienced a similar type of health-related crisis, even if separated by two thousand years. We are both church planters, venturing to new cities, sharing the gospel of Jesus and bringing new believers together to start churches. We have both experienced health infirmities that had the potential to halt our ministries. I guess if the apostle Paul had to deal with mysterious, ministry-threatening health issues, then I shouldn't be too surprised when I, a current-day church planter and pastor, must face a similar situation.

In the first century, Paul received a calling from God to take the eternity-altering good news of Jesus' death and resurrection from Jerusalem to the ends of the known world. He traveled thousands of miles, preaching the gospel at every opportunity and starting churches in at least fourteen different cities. To continue his powerful ministry he arranged rides on ships, hopped on carts, carriages, and caravans along trade routes and walked many, many miles. It's not hard to see that any kind of serious health problem would stop him in his tracks. So when he was struck with an unknown illness that he describes as "a thorn in my flesh" (2 Corinthians 12:7), it wasn't just his comfort that was at stake; this illness threatened the effectiveness of his ministry. If he couldn't travel, then he couldn't expand the reach of the gospel, and he couldn't visit the churches he started in order to encourage, instruct, and strengthen new Christians.

Yes, both Paul and I surely hoped to escape the discomfort of illness, but for both of us, something much greater was on the line—*our calling*.

Paul's first response was to pray. I think that is pretty standard when your health is in jeopardy and you have no idea what is going on. He says he prayed three times for God to remove his illness. When he says *three*, Paul doesn't literally mean he prayed three prayers; he is using the number symbolically to mean *thoroughly* or *completely*. Basically, he prayed and prayed and prayed until there was nothing left to say. Then he surrendered his requests to God and waited for a reply. And the Lord replied. The answer was no. Obviously this wasn't the response he had hoped for and naturally Paul would have felt confused. Why would God call him to a traveling ministry just to have him not be able to travel? Why would God give Paul the power to heal other people to display the power of Jesus just to have him not be healed himself? Paul doesn't record asking God any of these questions, but he does record God giving an explanation that allowed Paul to understand what God was doing and how he needed to respond. Jesus spoke to Paul and explained, "My grace is sufficient for you, for my power is made perfect in weakness" (2 Corinthians 12:9). I have come to learn that Jesus was basically saying, "I said no, and that's okay, because although I didn't remove the mountain in front of you, I am going to graciously give you the strength to climb it, and it will result in a glorious display of love."

Upon hearing Jesus' explanation Paul was given the wisdom to understand: "When I am weak, then I am strong" (2 Corinthians 12:10). Instead of concluding that his calling was over, Paul pivoted and found a new way to exercise his life's purpose. He reasoned that God was using this situation to help him avoid becoming conceited as his fame as a faith leader was increasing and he had to defend himself from some haters who wanted the influence he had. And he was inspired to a new ministry endeavor. Instead of traveling and speaking, he stayed put and started writing. This was no easy task. He wasn't able to just sit down at a craft coffeehouse and start a blog as he sipped a good pour-over coffee.[2] He didn't have a literary agent to line up a publisher for his Christian Living book. He couldn't even drop a letter off at the post office. None of those things were available. He would have to hunt down a scribe and a courier he could trust enough to travel hundreds of miles on his behalf to deliver the letter to the church he wanted to communicate with and then wait for their response.

That is exactly what Paul did.

First and Second Corinthians are written correspondence between Paul and the church he recently started in Corinth. We only have the record of what he wrote to the church, and not what the church wrote to him, so we have some gaps to fill in when Paul wrote, "Now for the matters you wrote about" (1 Corinthians 7:1). Not only did Paul and the church of Corinth slowly pass letters back and forth, but the Corinthian church also circulated Paul's letters around to other churches. Those letters became so influential in shaping the new movement of Jesus that they are now included in the canon of the Bible we read today. When you think about it, it really is okay that God said no to Paul's request for healing . . . it was more than okay. If God would have healed Paul, then Paul would have traveled to Corinth to speak directly with followers of Jesus to encourage and strengthen them. But it would have stopped there. Instead, because God didn't heal Paul, we all have access to his instruction and encouragement from the letters he wrote in lieu of being able to travel.

And it was Paul's words, written almost two thousand years ago, that God used to speak to me in my health crisis in a Dunkin' parking lot.

After receiving my diagnosis and coming to terms that my calling to pastoral ministry was going to be halted for some unknown period of time, I followed in Paul's footsteps. I prayed and prayed and

---

2. Like I'm doing right now.

prayed and asked God to make the cancerous tumor miraculously disappear. I have heard of it happening for others, so why not me?[3] After all, I was doing the Lord's work. People consider me *a good person* and when they hear of my situation, they ask, *Why do bad things happen to good people?* (more on that later). But after I had undergone a number of follow-up MRIs, the tumor still hadn't disappeared, and I had to schedule a second brain surgery followed by radiation and chemotherapy. I asked for healing, and God answered no—and that's okay because the Holy Spirit spoke to my heart in the Dunkin' parking lot. I heard the same words Jesus had spoken to Paul: "'My grace is sufficient for you, for my power is made perfect in weakness.'... For when I am weak, then I am strong" (2 Corinthians 12:9–10).

Paul reasoned that God would use his illness to guard him from pride. The Holy Spirit granted me insight in that moment to reason that God would use my illness to teach me the true meaning of strength and knit me together to my family with deep bonds of love. At this conclusion, my heart felt relief because deep down, I knew I needed this lesson.

We live in a culture that is contaminated with a warped idea of masculinity. As a follower of Jesus, I've been commanded to transcend cultural norms, ascribe to the values of God's kingdom, and allow Jesus to be my archetype of masculinity and strength. But I need personal tutoring by the Holy Spirit to correct my understanding of strength. At Dunkin', I began to see I had adopted the

---

3. For instance, while I was writing this chapter, I got a text from one of my best friends asking for prayers. His sister was scheduled for an MRI to examine a large lump they found in her breast. I prayed, as did many others, for a miraculous healing. The next day, I received the news that the large mass disappeared! The doctors couldn't explain it. But we all knew what had happened. Prayer works. So let me ask you a question: If you were in my shoes—if you had cancer and prayed that God would take it away but he said no and then you prayed that God would take away the cancer of a friend's sister and God graciously responded with a miracle—how would you feel? Elated or unfairly treated? In my case, it gave me confidence. It was further confirmation that God does hear our prayers and has the power to heal. So if God were to choose not to heal me, it would be okay because he must have a plan. I may not be able to fully see it yet, but he has always been good to me, so I can trust him now too. He said yes to her and no to me, and that's okay.

commercial idea of strength, which was weakening my most cherished relationships. Even later in life, my childhood neglect led me to believe I was on my own and that my strength was found in my independence.

My warped sense of strength was contributing to the walls I had constructed in my own heart that were keeping those I love the most at arm's length. My misunderstanding of strength had destroyed my ability to be truly vulnerable. I was fronting a facade of power and independence that was preventing me from making the courageous moves that would allow my loved ones to see me as I truly am. I was hiding behind a fake strength, and I welcomed God's correction, no matter how difficult it might be. But as the saying goes, "No pain, no gain." In this prayerful conversation with the Holy Spirit, my heart was enlightened to see that my diagnosis was not the undoing of a miraculous surgery; it was the continuation of the work God had already begun in my heart.

A Nudge toward the Impossible

I left Dunkin' and headed home. I no longer felt confused, but I still had another question. I prayed another pivotal prayer: *God, how can I cooperate?* This is one of the two most important prayers I've ever prayed, which you can pray at any time, good or bad:

1. *God, what are you doing?*
2. *How can I cooperate?*

I understood I was going to learn what was meant by *when I am weak, then I am strong* and that, somehow, to learn this would help me deepen my connection with my family. Now I wanted to understand how I could join God in his work on my soul. Out of nowhere came a memory from when I was ten years old. I was watching *Wide World of Sports* and saw for the first (and only) time an IRONMAN triathlon. I watched these elite athletes compete in an impossibly long triathlon, and thirty years later, I still think, *There's no way. These guys are superhuman. Who in the world can race 140.6 miles of swimming, cycling, and running . . . without taking breaks?* The idea of attempting this race never ever entered my mind. It was too far out of reach to even consider.

I got the sense that this IRONMAN memory from thirty years ago was no random memory. Instead, it was a nudge from the Holy Spirit to try something that seemed impossible . . . and to make the attempt in my weakest moment, proving to myself and all those watching that with God all things are possible. With him by my side, when I am weak, then I am actually strong.

My spiritual eyes opened to something else too. I could see a unique opportunity hiding in the devastating diagnosis of terminal cancer. I now had the opportunity to not just tell Hero about faith in Jesus but actually show her.

As a Christian father, *of course* I wanted to tell my child about Jesus. But now I could *show* her what true, resilient faith in Jesus looks like—that with God all things are possible. This was my chance to let my little girl see my weakness but also see me holding on to the hope of Jesus, believe in his promises, and find my strength in him as I press on to do what seems to be impossible. I couldn't think of anything more loving than to let her see authentic faith in a moment of severe crisis.

I pitched the idea to my wife: I was going to take on the IRONMAN competition while going through cancer treatment as a grand gesture of love for Hero and to teach her that with God all things are possible. And Natalie told me to go for it.

I never signed up for an easy life. When I placed my faith in Jesus twenty-five years earlier, I never believed he would make my life easier. From the start, I understood that Jesus lived a life of suffering, and that if I set out to follow Jesus, I'd likely be led into some significant suffering. Yet Jesus promised life to the full. That's what I signed up for when I trusted Jesus to lead my life.

Twenty-five years ago, I devoted myself to a meaningful life—a life lived to the full. The harder my life has become, the more meaningful it has become. How can we develop a full, meaningful life? We need to have something worth living for that is so precious we'd be willing to die for it. For the apostle Paul, it was introducing people to Jesus—people from his hometown all the way to those who live at the ends of the earth. For me, there is nothing I wouldn't sacrifice to show my daughter what strong, resilient faith looks like. Being diagnosed with cancer brought on a lot of pain and sadness, but it has also filled my life with meaning and purpose.

As I went on medical leave, I made a pivot with my life's purpose. For this next season, I would be focused not on leading and loving a church congregation, but instead on leading and loving my daughter by my example as I set out to learn about strength and endurance, weakness and vulnerability. I knew what I needed to do. I needed to sign up for a full-distance IRONMAN competition and start training immediately. That may sound crazy, and like quite a stretch, but I truly felt that this race was a calling from God. Let me explain the prayers that led me there.

Power Prayers

Years ago, I learned to pray two powerful prayers in tandem: *God, where are you working?* and *God, how can I join you?* I instinctively turned to these two prayers both in times of crisis and in times of calm. Meditating on these questions often allowed the Holy Spirit to show me opportunities I had never seen before. Routinely, they led me to experience spiritual growth when I had plateaued in my spiritual maturity. I learned these prayers from the bestselling author of *Experiencing God*, Henry Blackaby, and they changed the direction of my life. Don't wait for personal crisis to employ these power prayers. Take them before God now, and watch things begin to change.

God, where are you working? is a prayer of curiosity. It takes the focus off us and places God in the spotlight. As we open our spiritual eyes and survey where God may be at work around us, we also get to see God's character. Seeing God at work will reveal his values, priorities, passions, and heartbeat for the world. Experiencing God's character will inevitably change our character as we move toward him. As we begin to recognize his involvement in the here and now, our hearts will become more convinced of his desire to care for us and treat us with compassion.

God, how can I join you? is a prayer of connection that places us in a cooperative friendship with God, working with him to bring good into this world—even into our own souls. No longer will we be living our lives separate from God, hoping he will bless our own endeavors. Instead our actions will be intertwined with his, and we'll live with a sense of purpose that is bigger than ourselves.

Little did I know that this simple prayer would lead me to a grueling and inspiring race, even in the depth of my season of suffering. Little did I know that I was being called to be an IRONMAN with incurable brain cancer.

You can begin your power praying with something like this:

God, where are you working? What are you up to?

Allow time to meditate, and let God's Spirit direct your attention.

I want to see what you're doing and who you are. God, I want to experience you. Show me your heart and transform my heart.

Slow down and enjoy God's presence. Note how it feels to be united with God.

God, how can I join you? What can I offer? I want to cooper-
ate with you. How can I cooperate? Show me what gifts and
skills you have given me. It may not be much, but I want to be
with you in your work. Give me wisdom to discern my calling
in life.

Take a deep breath. You're safe in God's presence.

To be honest, joining you in your work is intimidating. I'm a bit
scared. Remind my heart that you are with me. Give me cour-
age and determination to do what you are calling me to do.
     In the powerful name of Jesus. Amen.

Continue praying in a similar way, uniquely crafting your prayer
to address each situation you find yourself in. In both crisis and
calm, regularly pray these power prayers. May they bring you the
same peace, discernment, direction, clarity, resolve, and strength
that they have brought me.

_____

The Lord replied. The answer was no.

_____

1. What happens when God answers no to a deep and appropriate desire of your heart? Is it possible to trust God when he says no to a legitimate and bold request?

    These are two of the most important prayers I have ever prayed, and you can pray them at all times, good or bad:

    - *God, what are you doing?*
    - *How can I cooperate?*

2. Consider how you can be curious about the work of God in your life and in the world around you. How can you create the necessary space to listen and to follow his Spirit?

CHAPTER 6

Do Difficult Things

Carry the fire.

CORMAC MCCARTHY

Discerning the voice of God is difficult. Misunderstanding him can be tragic.

I've already talked about hearing from God. I believe God spoke to my heart with divine insight in answer to my angry screams when my dad died. I believe God spoke to me at a Dunkin' parking lot by directing me to Scripture and impressing on my heart a prophecy of what he would teach me on the difficult road ahead.

I also believe that a random memory from childhood was a nudge from the Holy Spirit to attempt something crazy. This last assertion seems to be the most difficult for people to get behind. "Why would you attempt a megatriathlon to show your daughter that you love her? Aren't there a million other ways to show her your love?" Trolls on the internet said what a lot of people were thinking: *Obviously this guy did this for himself, not his daughter.* And I hate to admit it, but they're kind of right.

Everything we do has multiple motivations. Our desires are complex, and often two things can be true at the same time. But

80

what I've come to understand is that the primary motivation matters the most. Let me share my primary motivation for attempting IRONMAN, followed by all the secondary motivations I came to discover.

Primarily I wanted to learn what the Lord meant by promising that it is at my weakest moment that I am truly at my strongest. I wanted to teach this lesson to my daughter even as I was learning it. And I saw this as a grand gesture of love for her. Why is this a grand gesture of love? It is like writing someone's name in the dedication in the front of a book you poured your heart and soul into. It is like naming your child after someone you admire and hoping your child will mirror their character and likeness. It's like making a donation in someone's name to a cause that is dear to their heart. It's like planning a lavish party to celebrate someone and thinking through all the details and going to great lengths to display how sincerely you want that person to feel special.

For me, dedicating my race to my daughter was my way of saying to her that there was no distance I wouldn't go for her. I would never give up fighting through pain to be with her again. I'm willing to show her faith by example because her spiritual well-being means so much to me. She inspires me to find courage to try hard things and refuse to give up when things get tough.

I had plenty of other motivations as well, some of which showed up later and some that were there the whole time beneath the surface, waiting to be discovered. I knew I was facing a devastating fate, and I needed to stay positive. In the past, exercise has been the greatest antidote to my emotional depression. I knew my propensity to depression was going to be at an all-time high, so I wanted to increase the time I spent in exercise as well. I was told by doctors that exercise could help me fight off the side effects of radiation and chemo, especially fatigue.

Now, exercise is one thing; training for a 140.6-mile race is another. Did my excessive training cause more fatigue than a more moderate exercise plan? Probably. I have an all-or-nothing person-ality. If I would have planned to do a reasonable amount of exercise, would I have stuck to my plan and found the strength and steadfast-ness to get out of bed when my head was pounding and I was feeling nauseous and fatigued? Most likely not. Did I put an unfair amount of stress on my wife? Yes.

And I wish dearly that I would have done things differently—more on that later.

Another motivation was to find purpose in my pain and to live a storyworthy life. Now, I wasn't doing this to become well-known, have a documentary produced about me, and write this book. As a pastor, I've always felt that the term "celebrity pastor" was an oxymoron, and I've shied away from taking speaking engagements outside of my congregation. But I've always been driven to live a life of adventure and to accomplish things, as well as to live a unique life and take on challenges that can turn into good stories. And now I have a God-given story that I need to steward well—not for my glory, but for his. Which takes me back to hearing from God and learning to follow his leading.

Does this sound radical? I have never been a religious radical, but I have always wanted to authentically follow Jesus. As I read the Bible, I've noticed that the main point the early Christians were trying to get across to the people who had recently put their faith in Jesus is this: the focus is no longer on following rules; it's now on following the Spirit of Jesus. Obviously, if those who trust in Jesus are going to focus on following Jesus' Spirit, *we* are going to have to learn to hear his voice, identify his insights, and discern when he's nudging us in a certain direction. But it is not so obvious how to do that, and I still have a lot to learn.

I did not grow up in a religious household. My parents didn't point me to the need to hear the voice of the Spirit (and I suspect most parents don't give this gift to their kids). However, after twenty-five years of following Jesus and earnestly trying to figure out how to follow his Spirit, I've learned some things that can move me beyond the rules of religion. I've learned to do some things that may seem impossible without the help of God.

Here are four lessons I've learned that help me follow the Spirit and helped me decide that to compete in IRONMAN was one of God's callings on my life. Maybe they will be helpful for you too.

Four Ways to Discern the Voice of God's Spirit

First, I've learned that when a specific portion of Scripture comes to mind—one that seems to come out of nowhere—and is remarkably apt to my situation, I take it to be from the Spirit. I pay close attention to the words of that particular section of Scripture and pray for the Spirit to bring me an understanding that is beyond my own wisdom. Jesus promised that his Spirit would come as a gift to those who have put their trust in him and would remind us of Jesus' teaching (John 14:26). Jesus was originally explaining this to people who had spent a lot of time with him and heard him teach about many things concerning spirituality. For us, nearly two thousand years later, we have learned Jesus' teaching from the Scriptures. When a relevant Scripture comes to mind with an accompanying insight, for me it is the Spirit doing what Jesus promised. This is how I experienced the leading of the Spirit when I sat in my grief in the Dunkin' parking lot. My mind was led to 2 Corinthians 12:8–10. The Spirit was acting in accordance with Jesus' character, and this interaction cleared up my confusion and gave me direction (1 Corinthians 14:33).

Second, I've learned when a thought pops into my head that far exceeds the wisdom I've gained through experience, that thought is not from me but from the Spirit (1 Corinthians 2:12–14). I know quite well what my thoughts sound like. When a thought comes up that sounds much smarter than me, I *know* it's not me. Remember the story of my camping trip? After my dad died, I went to the desert to seek the Lord and find understanding because I couldn't comprehend why his life had ended so abruptly. I couldn't come up with an answer that satisfied my raging soul. After days of wrestling, I gave up and gave into my anger. At that point the Lord spoke—not in an audible voice, but by graciously imparting insight to my confused mind that settled my soul. I had tried for months to figure out why. When the answer finally came with satisfying clarity, I knew God was at work.

Third, the Scriptures teach that the Spirit brings peace and joy, especially in the midst of suffering (1 Thessalonians 1:6). I went to the desert to grieve my father's death because my soul was in tumult. I returned home at peace and even with a sense of joy at being reunited with God, my heavenly Father. I had spent months in grief counseling, which had helped some, but after sitting in my sorrow long enough, I hit a wall that therapy couldn't get me over. Only through an experience with the Spirit in the middle of intense suffering was I able to move beyond my sorrow. Concerning my cancer diagnosis, I arrived at the Dunkin' parking lot (it feels ridiculous to keep referring to a donut chain while I try to talk about serious spiritual issues!) feeling confused and uncertain. I left feeling at peace and even a bit joyful at the prospect of learning a new, deep truth that I had never been able to comprehend, even after years of talk therapy. As someone who battles depression, I didn't have it within myself to conjure up the emotions of peacefulness and joyfulness. I've learned that in situations like these, those emotions are made possible only through the Spirit.

Finally, I've come to see that one of the things I love most about receiving the gift of the Spirit is that I now have been given a power and love that can overcome fear and timidity (2 Timothy 1:7). I'm sure you can imagine how powerless I felt when I was told I was fighting a disease with no cure. I have never felt weaker than when I learned I had to fight for my life in a battle I had no chance of winning. I think it would be normal to feel abandoned by God and unloved in a moment like that. I would have expected to feel consumed by fear and determined to retreat. But I assure you that by the Spirit of God, I did not. I did not feel abandoned, unseen, or unloved by God. I did not feel like retreating out of a feeling of being powerless over my situation. Because of the experience I had with the Spirit, I believed God saw the very depths of my soul, that he came closer than I've ever felt before, and I felt emboldened to take a step forward instead of retreating. After I asked God, *What are you doing?*—and felt like the Spirit answered me—and when I then asked God, *How can I cooperate?* I felt so close to God, so loved by God, so empowered by the Spirit, and so emboldened that in my weakness, I felt I could attempt something I never would have believed I had the strength to complete on my own. I set my heart on completing IRONMAN in honor of my daughter.

Putting It All Together

Was IRONMAN a calling from the Spirit of Jesus on my life? Yes, I believe it was. All four lessons I had previously learned about discerning the Spirit converged in one decision. The Spirit had taken my mind to a Scripture that declared that God's power is best displayed in my weakness. And with this Scripture came two insights:

1. I need to learn what true strength is.
2. I have a unique opportunity to allow God's power to be displayed in my weakness in order that my daughter might see.

Every parent wants to teach their kids to dream big dreams because with hard work anything is possible. But I realized I was now able to teach not only that universal lesson, but I could teach my daughter an even more valuable lesson: when we chase our dreams, life will inevitably knock us down. But we can hold on to the hope of Jesus, stand back up in the strength of the Spirit, stay strong, and press on because with God *anything is possible*. The deeper lesson and the ability to identify it at that moment were way beyond me; this was insight beyond my years of wisdom—and it could come only from the Spirit.

I received the idea to attempt IRONMAN at my weakest as having come from the Spirit. I experienced a sense of profound peace. A tinge of joy developed into joy-fueled excitement. I felt God bringing purpose to my pain and significance to my suffering. As a result, I experienced unexpected peace and joy. Finally, setting my mind to testing God's promise felt empowering. Deciding to dedicate my race to my daughter felt incredibly loving. The decision to do IRONMAN as a grand gesture of love for my daughter felt like more than a crazy idea or even just a nudge from God; it felt like a calling on my life to which I could dedicate the next season of my life while I was on medical leave. Say what you will, but I am confident I heard a message from God and faithfully followed his leading.

To anyone who has discerned God's calling on their life, be sure of this: you *can* do difficult things. If you are frozen and can't seem to find the courage to take your first step, this simple technique can generate courage. Replace the word *afraid* with the word *excited*. Instead of saying, *I am afraid to* _____, say to yourself, *I am excited to* _____.

Fear and excitement feel similar. Switching the wording may help you discern if you want to attempt something scary. Reframing fear and excitement may be the thing that can finally get you moving. For example, instead of saying, *I'm afraid to quit my job*, say, *I'm excited to start a business*. Or instead of saying, *I'm scared to leave a relationship I've had for so long*, say, *I'm excited to learn to be okay on my own*. One last example: instead of saying, *I'm afraid to look stupid if I fail*, say, *I'm excited to learn something new*.

Of course you can't lie to yourself. You can't pretend you're excited about something when you're mostly just afraid. But if you can identify something that truly excites you in whatever it is you want to attempt, the thrill of possibility often will incite the action that fear has been blocking. Don't let the anxiety of misstepping cause you to miss out. There is strength in overcoming your fear of failure. Take a strong first step.

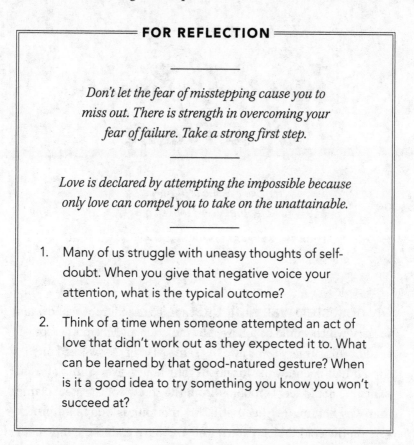

FOR REFLECTION

Don't let the fear of misstepping cause you to miss out. There is strength in overcoming your fear of failure. Take a strong first step.

Love is declared by attempting the impossible because only love can compel you to take on the unattainable.

1. Many of us struggle with uneasy thoughts of self-doubt. When you give that negative voice your attention, what is the typical outcome?

2. Think of a time when someone attempted an act of love that didn't work out as they expected it to. What can be learned by that good-natured gesture? When is it a good idea to try something you know you won't succeed at?

CHAPTER 7

There Is Power in a Name

In mine eye she is the sweetest
lady that ever I looked on.

WILLIAM SHAKESPEARE, *MUCH ADO ABOUT NOTHING*

My next step was difficult. I needed to endure a second brain surgery, which would be followed by radiation and chemotherapy.

For this surgery I was awake again as Dr. Berger worked on me. After I had been awake for about four hours, everything started to ache. I could feel throbbing from the screws of the steel clamp that was holding my head still. My motionless body had grown sore on the cold table. If you're tall and have endured a four-hour road trip in a compact car or a four-hour flight sitting in economy, you know what I'm talking about. Totally endurable while being uncomfortable. But during my surgery I felt especially tormented because I couldn't move at all. I couldn't shift to get more comfortable. I asked Dr. Berger if I could reposition my hips. He simply replied, "No." I had no choice but to stay still while my neurosurgeon removed my brain, piece by piece.

Eventually I heard him say, "Okay, we're done here." I thought he was talking to me. Looking back, I think he was talking to the anesthesiologist, who then put me back under—but not enough under. My skullcap was put back in, and then my scalp was stapled back together. In the process, I awoke to the sound of clattering metal as the staple gun fired. Dr. Berger is world-class; his anesthesiologist, not so much.

Feeling your scalp, which had been sliced open by a scalpel only hours before being stapled back together, hurts. The surgeon could tell I was in pain. He asked me if he should stop. As I look back, I think that was an odd question. But in the moment, I responded without hesitation, "Keep going." I desperately wanted the surgery to be finished—no delays!

———

After having the second brain surgery in San Francisco and taking two months to recover, my family and I relocated from California to Texas because I needed a specialized form of radiation that was offered at MD Anderson—and for some strange reason, my health insurance covered it without a fight. We got a long-term Airbnb and arrived in Houston in August. I was told that Houston was a great city to visit . . . except in August, when it had to have been the most humid place on the planet. Most Texans in that area dream about taking a vacation someplace comparatively cool—you know, like California. (As you get to know me, you'll see that I'm often found running full speed toward crazy situations.) So to Houston we went.

I started cancer treatment by immediately making a hard situation harder. Not only did I start treatment, but I also started training for a triathlon in that brutally humid Houston summer. On my first day of radiation and chemotherapy, I ran a mile. My head ached, my stomach was nauseous, and my sweat poured like never before in the gravy-thick summer air. One mile was a long way off from the marathon I'd need to complete. But it was a start. I had told my daughter I was going to train during treatment because I felt God had called me to such ridiculousness.

As I ran, feeling the agony in my body, mind, and spirit, I felt like a prophet of old who had followed God into ridiculous situations so he could use their life as an object lesson for the world. I hoped my life would become an illustration of faith for my daughter. But I had no idea if she'd be able to grasp what I was trying to accomplish—not a triathlon, but a faith that fully believed the Bible's words: "When I am weak, then I am strong." I wanted her to see that with God all things are possible.

On the second day of treatment, I ran two miles. I ran a little farther every day. I got a membership at an air-conditioned gym and hopped on the treadmill. Two miles became ten, and my pace was beginning to pick up—that is, until *it* happened.

A couple weeks into cancer treatment, I had a seizure while running. I had dialed in a ten-mile run on the treadmill, and something didn't feel right in my head. I got off the treadmill, sat with my back against the wall, and underwent a seizure—a moment that could prove to be the end of a dream. If my body could not manage a ten-mile run, how could I continue training for my 140.6-mile race in the not-so-distant future. This seizure could be seen as confirmation that I'd be crazy to attempt IRONMAN while undergoing cancer treatment.

The next day at my appointment, I told my doctors what had happened. I had already told them I was training for an IRONMAN. Up to this point, they were on board. When I initially told them about my aspirations, they encouraged me to exercise as much as my body was able. To be fair to my wife, who was concerned and didn't buy it when I told her the doctors thought that doing an IRONMAN was a great idea, I don't think the doctors knew how intense the training was going to be. And I think they assumed I was already a competitive triathlete whose body was used to endurance training.

Amazingly, when I told them I had had a seizure the day before when running ten miles, they didn't seem too concerned. They simply told me to back off a bit. The next day, I dialed down the pace on the treadmill and ran eleven miles. And I didn't have a seizure.

People often ask me what it feels like to have a seizure. Well, I can feel it coming, kind of like feeling a sneeze begin to build. But instead of the feeling being in my nose, it's in my brain. A sensory condition called an aura occurs before my seizure, and I feel like I'm starting to float. Then a wall of unavoidable energy comes at me and converges at the last second to hit me in the center of my being—right in the gut. It hits so hard I feel nauseated as the energy quickly dissipates out from the original stun grenade down toward my toes and up toward my brain.

As the energy goes down, I get weak in my knees but keep my balance. As the energy simultaneously goes up, my heart starts beating fast, as in a panic attack. When the energy finally reaches my brain, I have an out-of-body experience, with a strong sense of dread. Everything feels foreboding, and often I feel like someone is behind me. Or sometimes when someone is standing in front of me, I can feel threatened by them. I feel like I'm in danger while rationally understanding that nothing bad will happen. It feels similar to walking through a haunted house and looking at scary figures, but also understanding that they're just weird people who like to creep people out but aren't allowed to actually touch you.

I'm fortunate that my seizures don't cause me to pass out and convulse. Instead, I stay awake and aware. I experience the misfiring neurons in my brain and am able to remember how terrible and scary they feel. Sometimes, though, I wish I would pass out and have no memory of the event. But when a seizure occurs in a gym with all kinds of people around, I'm glad to be spared the horror of becoming a spectacle and terrifying other people. At this point in life, everything felt a little scary.

I would go to the treatment center every day and lie down on a futuristic slab of radioactive equipment. The medical team would firmly snap on a face mask of hard mesh plastic that would render my entire head unmovable. It always felt terribly claustrophobic to be held down, unable to move or even swallow. Then the radiation beam would be turned on and moved all around my head, with digital micro precision. Invariably, at about the two-minute mark, I'd be able to smell what I first thought was burning hair; in reality, it was my brain tissue burning in proximity to my olfactory glands.

The smell of my brain burning made me sick to my stomach every time I would undergo radiation. I would meditate to make it through, picturing God's hand intervening with even more precision than the greatest human technology could provide. I would envision God shielding healthy brain tissue from the gamma rays and reflecting all of them to the microscopic cancer cells randomly scattered throughout my brain—the cells the radiologist couldn't see, but God could. Then fifteen minutes later, the procedure would be over. I endured this routine for six weeks.

By the last day of my radiation, before heading back to California, I went to the gym and stepped on the treadmill one last time and ran twenty miles. That was by far the longest run I had ever done in my life and by far the most boring. There's a reason why treadmills are associated with the mindless, dull rat race of life. But during those twenty miles of going nowhere, I had plenty of time to reflect on the six weeks of radiation I had just endured.

I would feel nauseated every day and experience crippling fatigue brought on by a crushing headache. The radiation and chemotherapy were taking their toll with an intensity that was building each day. It would take everything inside me to get to the gym and train. I would run every day, and each day, I'd run a little farther. Why and how? I was a man motivated by a mission—to teach my daughter resilient faith. To be vulnerable enough to allow her to see me knocked down but also to be tenacious enough to get back up.

I had a calling on my life that gave me confidence as I prayed daily and asked God for strength. I had both *calling* and *confidence*, the two keys to resiliency. On my last run in Houston, I felt proud that I made it through radiation while starting chemo and that I progressed from one mile to twenty. Proud that I wasn't stuck in self-pity but was doing something out of love for my daughter.

Learning to Swim

My family and I flew home to California. The summer of 2019 had come and gone, and fall had arrived. Natalie, Hero, and I were ready to leave the humidity of Houston and move back into our house in Orange County. As we were getting ready to go to the airport, as I was lifting a featherlight bag of Hero's stuffed animals into the car, I threw out my back. I couldn't get up off the ground, and Natalie couldn't lift me. We didn't know many people in town, but luckily the woman we knew best was once a NCAA Division 1 basketball player. She came over, picked me up, put me in the car, and slipped me some muscle relaxants. I was able to hobble onto the plane. I was so beat (and medicated) that I passed out on the plane and had a pleasant flight back.

The medical team had just cranked up my chemotherapy, which leads to muscle strains, so it took me longer to recover than usual. Fortunately for me, swimming was an excellent way to rehab my back. It was also the next discipline I needed to learn. I arrived back in California where the sun was shining and the air was warm enough to spur me to want to get into the cool water of the outdoor Olympic training pool just down the street.

When my back healed enough for me to drive, I went to the pool and paid two dollars to swim at noon with the senior citizens. I went to the locker room, changed into my Speedo (a piece of clothing I hadn't worn since college when I traveled to France), and walked out to the pool deck.

I looked around at all the seventy-year-old wrinkly skin and noticed something. These people knew how to swim *properly*. I did not. Trying to fake it till I make it, I stood at the edge of an open lane and shook my arms out like Michael Phelps. I opted out of stepping up to the starting platform and instead hung my toes over the edge of the concrete coping. *Here goes nothing.* I dove in, and the coolness of the water enveloped my skin. I swam under water as long as I could and then surfaced . . . discouragingly close to where I had jumped in. I gulped for air, stuck my face into the water, and tried to move my arms gracefully. I tilted my head to the side, trying to take a breath, but got a mouthful of water. Coughing, I came upright and started treading water.

Before I was really ready, I put my face back into the water and tried that graceful charade all over again. My awkwardness caused me to work overtime, but eventually I made it to the end. One length of the pool. I was exhausted after *one length*. I was going to need to be able to do *seventy-five more lengths* in a pool. I needed to turn 50 meters into 3,800. And I was going to have to do it in the ocean, fighting waves and currents. How on earth was I going to do that? It seemed impossible.

I needed help. Fortunately, one of my friends had once been a college swimmer until a shoulder injury ended his career. He once even swam against Michael Phelps but lost, just like every other swimmer who has competed against Phelps—though Travis claims it was "by a small margin."

Travis started coming to the pool to coach me. Each time he got in the pool with me, he outswam me by an enormous margin. He would laugh at how slowly I moved through the water and how my body seemed to sink as I swam. Then he'd shout at me from the side of the pool and tell me the same things over and over. I was a slow learner. But he stuck with me and kept making me go farther than I thought I could go. When my arms were jelly, he told me to sprint half a length. I didn't even know that sprinting in a pool was a thing. I hated sprinting.

After training for months, I was swimming a mile. However, a mile isn't 2.4 miles. I'd hit a wall at a mile. Every time I got there, I would hit a mental and physical barrier. Despite the frustration and discouragement, I began to really appreciate my time in the water. I enjoyed stretching out for each stroke and being in cool water with the warm sun on my back. My watch kept track of my laps so I was able to let my mind wander and my thoughts come freely. I thought of my daughter. I thought of her name.

Hero Renee Hewitt. She shares my last name and my sister's middle name—a person I hope she resembles. People make assumptions about her first name and about Natalie and me who named her. We made the mistake of telling people what we planned to name her before she was born. Family members urged us to reconsider the name Hero. They told us that kids might make fun of her and that she might resent us in the future. I imagine they might have rolled their eyes at us behind our backs. Around 2015, many parents, especially from California, were getting a bad rap for giving their kids bizarre names. To us the name wasn't strange at all.

Hang in there for a minute while I geek out a little. Natalie is a professor; I'm a pastor. Natalie wrote her PhD dissertation on William Shakespeare's influence on the Gothic novel. I was familiar with multiple theories of Christian redemption. Hero is a female character in Shakespeare's play *Much Ado about Nothing.* The climax of the play involves Hero's supposed death, which would reconcile broken families and restore love. Fitting, right? It's also a bit snobbish. To be honest, I would have had no clue that Hero is a Shakespearean character if I hadn't asked Natalie, "Would you ever want to name our child after a Shakespearean character?"

If you're a real intellectual snob, you're judging me for not knowing that Hero is actually a name from Greek mythology that Shakespeare stole/borrowed for his play. And you would be correct for judging my ignorance. Natalie also had to inform me of the history of our daughter's name. The Greek myth actually captivates my heart more than Shakespeare's use of the name—so much so that I have a tattoo depicting a scene from the myth. Hero loves looking at it and tracing it as I tell her the story.

The myth of Hero goes like this: Hero was a beautiful young woman with gorgeous hair. (I prayed that our daughter would inherit her mom's hair, and God granted that request.) Hero was incredibly beautiful—a beauty I see in my daughter—so beautiful that even the gods wanted to possess her and call her their own. But Hero was chaste and resisted them. A mere mortal man named Leander genuinely loved her, and she loved him. (I pray that our daughter will see through power and prestige and give her heart only to someone willing to truly love her.)

For some reason, Hero lived across a vast sea in a tower. (I could google this for accuracy, but that's the beauty of a myth told orally and passed down, changing slightly over time—details just get in the way!) She lived apart from Leander, her love, and yet Leander refused to let distance separate him from Hero.

One night, Leander began to swim across the sea and confronted a multitude of dangers along the way. The weather turned bad, and while fighting against the elements and the jealous gods who were trying to pull him down into the underworld, the wind blew out the light from Hero's tower, thus extinguishing his guiding light. Leander wandered through the sea until he became exhausted, but he kept forging ahead.

I've heard two possible conclusions to this myth: (1) Leander drowned and washed up onto the shore, where Hero discovered his body, and (2) Leander made it out alive and reunited with Hero.

I prefer, of course, the ending where the lovers are united and live "happily ever after." (I pray for a happy ending in love for my daughter.) The tragic ending has always bothered me—until one day as I swam and meditated on this story. I connected for the first time with the tragic ending. Here's why.

It seemed impossible to go the 2.4 miles that's required for an

IRONMAN swim. I have heard a bunch of stories about people who entered IRONMAN competitions multiple times and never made it past the swim. I wondered if I would be that person. And yet, whether or not I was able to go the distance, I could now see that love isn't declared by *completing an attempt* but by finding the courage to *make the attempt* for the sake of our love. Love is declared by attempting the impossible because only love can induce us to take on the unattainable.

Just as Leander was compelled by love to attempt an impossible swim, I was embarking on a feat I wasn't sure I would complete. As I considered the alternative ending—the tragic one—of Leander's failed attempt, my heart was moved for the first time by love expressed in failure. My soul was emboldened, and I was empowered to overcome the fear of failure.

My body, which had been battered by two brain surgeries, thirty radiation treatments, and high-dose chemotherapy, might not be able to endure such a long swim. Failure was a very real possibility. Even if my body couldn't come through, my love would be on display as I strove to make it. As my brain kept fighting encroaching cancer cells, it might not be able to stave off recurring tumors. The medical experts have told me I can't win this fight without a major breakthrough in treatment research. *But I will fight.* I will give my all to be with Hero and Natalie for as long as I can. Even if I ultimately lose my fight, I hope a tragic ending will not only result in sorrow but will have the warm glow of love.

After we moved back to California, I was glad to see that kids at school didn't make fun of Hero's name but rather were excited to meet someone named Hero. The name stuck in their minds and helped her make friends. I'm glad she is an extrovert. If she were shy, I think the naysayers would be right; she would probably hate the attention the name brought. Our backup plan was to call her Ro or Renee. However, she is happy with Hero. I love the story of her name on so many levels.

After a great meditation session in the water, I grew tired and stopped swimming. I checked my watch, and I could hardly believe that I had gone a mile and a half—well past the one-mile mark. I gained the confidence that if I just kept on training, I would learn to go the distance. Hero's name gave me the tenacity needed to break through the wall.

There is power in a name.

The Strength of a Name

Names matter. Even if we name our kids whatever sounds coolest to us, the names we ascribe matter. My parents named me Jason. Why? I don't know. But I do know that Jason was the most popular boy name in the 1980s. *A lot* of other kids in my school had the name Jason. What's more, three kids on my block were named Jason. I was the youngest, so everyone started calling me Jay. My name didn't seem to have much significance to my parents.

Names matter to God. God knows my name, and he knows your name as well. He knows you, sees you, and cares for you. And no matter whether your name is a generic one or a trendy one, God himself will give you a new, precious name for eternity.

Throughout the Bible, we find accounts where God changed people's names to reflect his purposes for them. God changed Abram's name to Abraham, Sarai to Sarah, Jacob to Israel. Names create meaning. When God first appeared to Moses, Moses asked God to tell him his name. God responded by introducing himself as Yahweh, a Hebrew name that means "I Am Who I Am." Names stand for the essence of a person. God declared to Moses that not only has he existed from the beginning of time; he *is* existence. Yahweh is life itself.

God commanded Joseph and Mary to give the child whose birth was about to happen the name Jesus—from the Hebrew *yeshua,* which means "the LORD saves." Jesus was born with a purpose—to save his people from their sins (Matthew 1:21), so that now "everyone who calls on the name of the Lord will be saved" (Romans 10:13). And Jesus promises this: "You may ask me for anything *in my name*, and I will do it" (John 14:14, emphasis added).

Jesus' name is powerful. His name has power because of who he is. So the next time you pray to God, be confident that you are welcomed into his holy presence because you come in the name of Jesus. You can ask boldly because you're asking in the power of the name of Jesus. When you pray in the name of Jesus, things change and you grow. There is power in a name.

Months after breaking through the mile barrier in the water, I was finally able to swim 2.4 miles comfortably. As the race got closer, I was now training in open water. I learned that especially in open water, you shouldn't swim alone. I typically trained with my friend, who was also training for an upcoming IRONMAN event.

One day, he couldn't be there. The weather was bad. The fog was thick, the water cold. As I swam away from shore, I began to feel the pull of the current. I kept pressing on, but something didn't feel right. I stopped and started treading water so I could look back toward the shoreline and see how far I had gone. The problem was that I couldn't see the shore through the fog. I couldn't see more than ten feet in any direction. I was nervous. But I knew I hadn't swum more than a half mile, so I knew I had plenty of energy in the tank.

I pointed myself in the direction of where I thought the sand should be, and I started swimming. I lifted my head and looked for the shore every so often, but I saw nothing. I kept swimming. My watch was telling me I had gone more than a mile. I had more energy left in the tank but I wasn't sure whether I had been turned around by the current. It was possible I was a mile and a half away from shore, which would mean, at the very least, that I would need to swim a total of three miles to make it back. This thought came into my mind: *Huh, I've always wondered how it is that a grown man could drown. Now I understand.* I still had energy, but I knew I wouldn't forever. I had no idea where I was.

I thought of Leander. Months earlier in the pool, I imagined myself as Leander in a figurative way. Now I was relating to him quite literally. In an angry episode of irony, I was furious at the possibility that I would die while training for a triathlon instead of from the effects of brain cancer.

I prayed. I swam. I prayed. I planned to float on my back once I started to get tired. I thought of Hero. I swam. I prayed. Then the thick fog started to burn off, and I spotted the shore. It wasn't far away. I still had energy and had made it out of the rip current. I swam to shore and decided to forgo the long ride I had planned and drove home instead. *What an idiot!*

I wish I would have better assessed the risk of swimming alone in bad weather. I was lucky to make it back to shore. That day taught me a valuable lesson. I am learning that risks must be assessed before accepted. Life is full of frightening circumstances and unavoidable risks. Many times we don't have much control when it comes to the risk facing us; other times it's completely up to us if we're going to take a risk or pass on pursuing a potential pitfall. Starting a business, accepting a new position, leaving a relationship, moving out of state, checking into rehab, speaking up for yourself, or any situation that can lead us through uncertainty will confront us with risk.

When you decide an opportunity is worth the risk, expect to have to overcome some adversity—that's the adventure of it. Realize there are multiple ways to accomplish your calling. Be wise, and take the route that is most likely to get you to your destination intact.

Risks must be assessed before accepted.

*Life is full of frightening circumstances
and unavoidable risks.*

1. Is your tolerance for risk high or low? Do you feel your
    relationship with risk needs adjustment?

2. Where do you typically turn to find a sense of security
    in times of uncertainty?

CHAPTER 8

Training through the Apocalypse

*It is not surprising a lot of people have given
up competing altogether and gone to sit in the
grandstand, eat junk food and shout abuse.*

BANKSY, *WALL AND PIECE*

Training was hard. Then it got harder.

I suffered a seizure and a back strain while training for the run.
I battled fatigue and nausea as I awkwardly learned to swim. And
then I hopped on the bike. I assumed, probably just like *you* would
assume, that biking would be the easiest of the three triathlon
sports. I figured every kid can ride a bike. I soon discovered that I,
too, can ride a bike—but only for about 25 miles; not *112*. I like beach
cruisers. They're slow and fun. I do not like road bikes, especially
if they have triathlon bars. Triathlon bars look impressive because
they look aggressive. But I learned that aggressive in the cycling
community is all about putting your body into angles that require a
magical skill called *flexibility*.

I am not flexible, and that has absolutely nothing to do with cancer. When I was in elementary school, we did something called the Presidential Fitness Test. (I wanted so badly to earn the certificate signed by President George H. W. Bush!) All I needed to do was (among a few other things, such as push-ups and a fifty-yard dash) run a mile in under eight minutes, do six pull-ups, and then sit and reach thirty centimeters toward my toes. A one-mile run in under eight minutes—no problem for a kid fueled by anxious energy. Six pull-ups—I weighed sixty pounds, so my chin basically floated over the bar. But the "sit and reach" was menacing. I sat down and extended my freakishly long ostrich legs. The thirty centimeters on the board looked a hundred miles away. I gave it my all. My hamstrings were on fire, and I was nowhere close to stretching far enough to win the award. But I was obsessed, so I asked my teacher if I could try again. On the next try, I had my friend push on my back, and as I let out a yell, I barely made it to the thirty-centimeter line. But I did it and got the certificate, even if later in life, I may have it revoked on an interference technicality. So, yes, I have never been flexible.

Cycling requires flexibility. You need flexible hamstrings, flexible hips, and a flexible back—none of which I had. By this time, my lungs and heart could handle cycling, but at about twenty-five miles, my tendons have had enough. I aimlessly and endlessly stretched at home. It did not help. After four or five attempts at cycling more than twenty-five miles, my body said, *Nope. No more of this.* I was finishing a ride, and as I got off the bike and swung my foot over the seatpost, my whole body crumpled up, I made a very strange sound from the pit of my being and went down. I had thrown out my back before, but never like this.

I was sidelined, and I was depressed. I was stuck in my negative thoughts: *At its best, my body isn't athletic enough to handle the cycling portion of the race, and the cramping from chemo is not helping. The chemo is making my back recovery take forever, and I'm falling behind on my training schedule. I'm not going to be prepared enough to even attempt the race. This was a stupid idea.*

While I couldn't train, I had time to research, which made my mindset even worse. As I looked into various training programs, I realized that my progress was way slower than a typical athlete who was training for IRONMAN. As I explored how to read my lab results, I discovered that my low white and red blood cell counts were the result of the chemo killing every cell that divides rapidly—cells that are responsible for carrying oxygen to the muscles.

All of a sudden, things clicked. A famous endurance athlete was caught blood doping (having his blood removed, stored in a refrigerator, and then transfused back into his body during races—multiplying the amount of oxygen-carrying blood cells in his body).[1] I, on the other hand, was anti-doping. My oxygen-carrying blood cells were being destroyed, and I was training (and soon racing) with a deficiency of oxygen in my muscles. No wonder my progress was so painfully slow. *This was a stupid idea.*

Eventually my back healed. A month had passed, and I had become very discouraged. I was missing the euphoric chemicals my body was producing during training. I knew I would benefit from intense exercise during training, and now I knew just how depressing it was to go without. I started training again.

I think the rest did me well. I got serious about overcoming my flexibility issues by doing an extensive warm-up and cooldown routine every day, as well as doing yoga most nights before bed. And sure enough, I started making progress in my cycling. By the end of 2019, I had gone from only being able to bike twenty-five miles to being able to do fifty miles. An accomplishment, to be sure, but still a long way off from the 112 miles I had to work up to.

At this point, I was proficient enough in all three athletic disciplines, and it was time to start combining them, in what is

---

1. See Benjamin Wedro, "Blood Doping," MedicineNet, www.medicinenet.com/blood _doping/views.htm, accessed May 10, 2023; Brit McCandless Farmer, "The 60 Minutes Report That Helped Reveal Lance Armstrong Doping," CBS News, May 25, 2020, www .cbsnews.com/news/lance-armstrong-doping-60-minutes-2020-05-25.

called *brick training*. Brick training entails doing a swim workout, immediately followed by cycling, or a long cycling workout followed by a run. It was at this point I realized just how far out of my league I was. And it was then that I received the grace I needed.

Finding the Help You Need

The sport of triathlon has a man of myth and legend whose name is "One Arm" Willie Stewart. He is a four-time IRONMAN finisher, competing at the highest level—the IRONMAN championships in Kona, Hawaii. How on earth could he swim 2.4 miles through the big surf in the open waters of Kona with only one arm? How did he develop the mindset to even try? How was he able to persevere and succeed? I knew I had to talk with him.

I heard a rumor that he trained at a YMCA in Boise, Idaho. While visiting my in-laws for Christmas in Idaho, I tracked him down. In stalker-like fashion, I took the opportunity permitted by a lazy afternoon with family and headed to the local YMCA. I walked down a back hallway and saw an office door with his nameplate on it. I entered the room, and a woman was sitting at his desk. I asked her where I could find Willie, and she hesitantly told me where he had been training. I searched the name of the gym on my Google Map app and drove across town. He wasn't there either, but everyone in Boise knows who Willie Stewart is. I found someone who was willing to give me his phone number.

That afternoon, I called his cell phone. When he answered, he told me he was on a chairlift, spending the day skiing. I told him a bit about my goals and asked if he'd be willing to grab coffee. He kindly offered to meet up the next morning. As we sipped coffee, he answered all my rookie questions and addressed my aspirations. At one point he looked at me and said, "You're going to do this. I'm going to help you get there. I don't exactly know how, but I'm going to help you get to the finish line."

The year 2019 came to a close and 2020 began. One-Arm Willie and I kept in touch, and he soon became a friend and a huge source of inspiration. If he could do it, I could do it. One bright and crisp January morning in California, I was talking to Willie on the phone and he said, "You know, I was talking about you the other day when I was on a run with my friend. She has competed at the world championship level of IRONMAN. She's a cancer survivor and is now coaching athletes. I'd like to introduce you to Margaret Hepworth."

By connecting me with Margaret, Willie fulfilled his promise to me to help me reach the IRONMAN finish line despite my limitations. During my first conversation with Margaret, it became clear that she knew a lot and that I didn't. Not only did she have expertise in triathlon training, but she also knew firsthand the harsh effects of cancer treatment on the body. She could tell I desperately needed help if I was going to have a chance at finishing IRONMAN. Margaret offered to coach me. Knowing the financial impact of cancer treatments, she offered to coach me for free. Her invaluable coaching saved me in many ways.

Margaret designed a specific training plan for me. There was no way around it—competing in IRONMAN takes intense training and a giant load of physical stress on one's body. Margaret never lost sight of the fact that I was still recovering from a second brain surgery and thirty-five radiation treatments, as well as undergoing a current regimen of high-dose chemotherapy.

Taking into account my time and health limits, Margaret designed a plan that would at least get me to the starting line. She monitored my progress via my smartwatch and training app. We talked on the phone every week, and she adjusted my workouts, depending on how my chemo-crushed body was handling the workload.

Margaret also imparted wisdom. She reminded me, "This is supposed to be fun." She urged me, "Be kind to yourself." She told me over and over, "The hardest part of IRONMAN is getting to the starting line healthy." Because she had been in my shoes, both as an athlete and as a cancer fighter, she knew how much she could push me without breaking me. I listened and did what she told me to do. She pushed me, and the workouts were hard. All of my health issues were still there, but now I had a coach helping me navigate those challenges. Even though I had never met her face-to-face, I leaned on her more than anyone. I needed her.

Historic Hardships

Training was hard, and then it became nearly impossible. I was training in 2020. When the COVID-19 pandemic hit the United States early that year, it made everything harder for everyone. I could no longer train with the friends who pushed me and walked alongside me. Some of the training facilities shut down. But what made training unbearably difficult was the stress it put on my family.

When I began training for IRONMAN, I dropped off Hero at school, while Natalie went to work at her university and I trained. I was on medical leave, and the circumstances seemed ideal for attempting something that required a ton of time. When the pandemic hit and California schools shut down in March 2020, Hero was suddenly at home, while Natalie was working from home *and* taking care of Hero—and I was gone. Natalie took over Hero's playroom and set up a home office / video recording studio to broadcast her lectures remotely to her students. Hero, bored and missing her school friends, was frustrated and begged her mom to give her back the playroom.

The power struggle between mother and daughter was intense, and so was my training regimen. At this point I was training at high milage—more than one hundred miles most days. When Natalie would wake up, I was already gone, leaving her on her own. Hero wondered where I was all day. I had started this endeavor to bring my family together. Now it was pulling us apart. I wondered if I had misunderstood God's calling on my life. I considered quitting. I was stuck.

Natalie was talking with her boss and decided to be honest and let him know how difficult life felt at the moment. She told him about my treatments and my training. When he heard how often I was away from home, he astutely asked, "Does it feel like you've already lost him? Like he's gone already?" The idea of premature grief struck a chord deep inside of her. She kept this to herself until after the race, when I asked her directly about what this moment in life was like for her. I was cut to the heart.

My intended grand gesture of love for Hero was making Natalie feel unloved. Nat and I were fighting a lot, and I wanted to bring resolution. I had made a promise to Hero, and I didn't want to break it. I thought I had a calling on my life, but I now doubted if I was discerning God's leading correctly. I had to make an impossible decision. Natalie felt as if she had no agency to ask me to stop my pursuit of IRONMAN. She later told me, "When I initially said yes, I didn't know what I was getting into. I often thought to myself, *Well, I said yes, so* ... I had no choice. I couldn't keep a dying man from his dream. I felt like I shouldn't have made things harder for you. And I began to feel like I was another obstacle in your way." I knew I had lost her support. But at that point I didn't know what to do. I kept training.

The emotional stress was heavy. Cancer was weighing me down. And then I got word on March 7, 2020, that IRONMAN Australia was canceled because of the COVID-19 pandemic. I was devastated. I had been super excited to race in Australia because I knew it would be a memorable experience. Beyond the breathtaking beauty of Australia, it was home to koalas—Hero's and Natalie's favorite animals. They loved how cuddly the sleepy animals were. Near Port Macquarie, the city where the race was to be held, was a magical koala sanctuary where people could interact with the animals as part of the animals' rehabilitation process.

One of Natalie's good friends lived just an island away. We had once visited her on New Zealand's North Island while on our honeymoon, and I was looking forward to returning as a family. In Australia, the race was slated to travel through picturesque landscapes and the family memories we'd create would be as golden as the coastline. But that dream ended when I opened the email. I clenched my jaw and walked away from my laptop and went for a run.

The next day, I returned to my computer and transferred my registration to another race in Northern California. No one in my family was particularly excited about the new location. That race was soon canceled too, and the next one as well. Each cancellation was like a blow to the stomach. If the stress on my family and health hadn't been a clear enough message that this idea was ill-advised and unwise, now each race I registered for was taken away from me. Should I read the writing on the wall, accept the reality, and walk away? I could not. I registered for a race in Florida, not sure if it would be canceled, like all the others before it. And so I continued training for a race that most likely wouldn't happen.

Judge me if you would like. I can't put into words exactly why I decided to keep moving forward. But I did. IRONMAN became a metaphor of sorts, a physical display of a spiritual principle: When I am weak, then I am strong. I hoped that my being able to cross the finish line would serve as a reminder to Hero that when life knocks us down, we must hold on to the hope of Jesus. We need to rise up in the strength of Jesus, stay strong, and press on because all things are possible through the strength Jesus provides.

Even with the pain my family had been experiencing due to my training, I felt like I couldn't let Hero see me give up and break the promise I had made to her. I was determined to not abandon the calling I believed God had placed on my life for that particular season. I pressed on toward the goal, and it was the hardest thing I've ever done in my life.

The summer of 2020 saw a record heat wave in California. I was training triple-digit miles in triple-digit heat. Then wildfires started burning. In that year, nearly ten thousand fires burned nearly five million acres across California, creating the biggest wildfire season in its history. That summer, the sky was red all day. Ash rained down and covered everything. The suffocating summer atmosphere was unhealthy. Health alerts were issued, advising the area's residents not to exercise outdoors. To get to the starting line, I'd have to train through the apocalypse.

Am I stubborn or determined? Narcissistic or devoted? I don't know, but I didn't quit. I considered it and talked to those I trusted most, but in my heart, I knew I couldn't give up in my heart. And so I kept training.

New Innovations

I was barely holding on, and then I had a phone conversation with the media director at IRONMAN. At this point, I was an honorary IRONMAN Foundation athlete—not because of my speed, strength, or stamina, but simply because of my story. IRONMAN is always looking for athletes who embody their motto: *Anything is possible*—and that was me. This honorary status allowed me access to staff members at IRONMAN.

I was given some inside information. IRONMAN had decided to cancel all of their events worldwide, including the world championships in Kona, Hawaii—the first time the world championships had ever been canceled. But the people who work for an organization that really believes anything is possible don't simply give up. Instead, they decided to respond to a first-time cancellation by taking a step into the future. They shared with me that on October 9, 2020, IRONMAN would hold its first-ever full-distance virtual race—the historic IRONMAN VR world championships.

And they asked me if I would agree to participate and be featured in the competition. Before race day, they would create an athlete spotlight—a montage of footage with me training, interacting with family, and sharing with the digital audience the reason for taking on the IRONMAN challenge. They'd also send their media team to follow my progress live during the race. Then on the next morning, they'd interview me live after the race had ended. I was tempted to jump at the opportunity and agree right then and there while on the phone, but I'm glad I didn't.

The offer was enticing because it tapped into a childhood dream of mine. More than anything, in junior high I wanted to be a sponsored rollerblader. It was the early 1990s, and the extreme sports scene was on the rise. Yes, I was aware that skateboarding, surfing, snowboarding, and motocross were all way cooler than rollerblading. Some even thought, though it was surely open to debate, that even the bodyboarding spongers were cooler than us rollerbladers. But I didn't care. I lived in Yucaipa, California, where it was too hot for ice hockey, and even if a rink had been nearby, no one would have the money to play.

So I was all about roller hockey in the street. And roller hockey morphed into freestyle rollerblading, which became an obsession and a way to escape my home. I was never extreme enough to go pro, but I dreamed of being sponsored and receiving free skates from Roces and free wheels from Kryptonics, as well as appearing in the *Daily Bread* magazine (a publication for aggressive bladers). Why did I want this so badly? I have no idea. It wouldn't have made me cool or rich. I guess when you're twelve, nothing you do makes sense and you like what you like without any logical reason or concern about street cred.

Dreams hide in the back of our hearts for a lifetime. My heart leaped with preteen glee when IRONMAN began sending me free gear, like I was some kind of big-time athlete or something. They sent me a ROKA wet suit and a couple pairs of Hoka One One shoes. A Trek retailer gave me a bike I could never have afforded. Again, I thought back to my ten-year-old self who saw IRONMAN for the first time on CBS's *Wide World of Sports*. I was in awe of the elite athletes on the broadcast. They seemed superhuman. The thought never crossed my mind that I could ever do something like IRONMAN. Now, not only was I going to attempt the megatriathlon, but I was also going to be a featured athlete. Of course I knew I wasn't an elite athlete. I wasn't trying to win the race; I was just aiming to finish it. But it was fun to pretend. I *so* badly wanted to be a featured athlete in IRONMAN's VR race.

There was a catch. Athletes pay a ton of money to race organizers because it takes a lot of work to organize an IRONMAN race. To do a virtual race would mean I'd have to take on a considerable amount of work. I had never done an IRONMAN before, not even one of their smaller, shorter races. I had no idea what to expect when it came to the logistics of the race. I was just planning to show up with my gear and give it my all. Now I was going to have to plan everything.

Coming Home

This is how IRONMAN's historic, first-ever full-distance and *virtual* triathlon worked: athletes from all over the world would register with IRONMAN for the race, download the official app, and sync it with an approved sports watch that would track distance, elevation, speed, and time. It was each athlete's responsibility to plan their own 140.6-mile course, taking into account both traffic and elevation change; essentially, you couldn't plan a downhill course. Also, each athlete would have to figure out how to set up aid stations along the way so they could refill their water bottles and grab some nutrition. Finally, at some point on the weekend of October 9–11, 2020, all the registered athletes would begin their races and try to go the distance without seeing the other athletes against whom they were competing.

That is a lonely 140.6 miles with a lot of logistics—any of which could go completely awry.

I considered all these logistics and realized why IRONMAN had never attempted a full-distance virtual race before. I ended the phone call by saying, "Let me talk to my wife"—which is married-man code for no.

True to my word, I talked to Natalie about it. IRONMAN had put so much strain on our family. I was nervous to bring it up. She surprised me. She told me it was sweet that my original plan was to race in Australia so the trip could be a family vacation. She said she loved the idea that I wanted to visit the koala rehab center so she and Hero could cuddle their favorite animal of all time.

And then Natalie added that the romantic[2] idea of going to Australia would have undoubtedly posed challenges, and that for her it was less stressful to think about doing the race in our own hometown. In her wisdom, she pointed out that by planning our own course, more of our friends and church family could be there to support us. She told me about the day I was out training and Hero wanted to set up a blanket on the front lawn so she could wave to me as I came by the house on my usual run route. When she painted the picture of placing the finish line in front of our home, my heart was filled with significance as I considered the metaphor of racing home to my family. I knew I'd give it my all to make it home to them, even if I wasn't sure my body would be able to accomplish the feat.

I called IRONMAN and told them I was in. We called our good friend Brittany, who is extraordinarily proficient at mobilizing people for a cause. She is simply amazing. We asked if she would mobilize our friends and church community to help set up and staff the aid stations. She rounded up two hundred people to pitch in. She arranged an opening ceremony where I would start the race in a wedding venue gazebo overlooking the Pacific Ocean at the Newport Dunes Waterfront Resort. She asked Jon Juroe, a contractor friend

---

2. To my professor wife, the word *romantic* does not mean "sweep me off my feet," but rather "unreasonable."

of ours, to construct a re-creation of IRONMAN's iconic structure that would hold up the official finishing tape that IRONMAN would be sending out to us. Brittany thought through every detail, even arranging a chase vehicle staffed with Kane Johnson, a paramedic and engineer with the Huntington Beach Fire Department; Jon Ankenman, a bike tech; and Corrie Mattson, a professional photographer.

While Brittany built a team of supporters, I kept working toward my goal. By the end of September 2020, I was finally able to swim two miles, ride a hundred miles, and run twenty miles. I was terrified to try to do it all in one day in under seventeen hours. I had never even run a marathon before. I couldn't imagine starting a marathon after already racing 115 miles of swimming and cycling, but I had to try. I had no doubt I was surrounded by a strong community of people who love me. Without these saints—other followers of Jesus—I'd have had no chance to set out to accomplish what I felt God had called me to do. I was overwhelmed with gratitude.

Strength in Community

Down through the years, I've learned that finding the strength to overcome adversity and the courage to press on is exponentially multiplied by the support of the community of saints. When people believe in us enough to rally behind us, our spirits are encouraged and our hearts are filled with boldness. I've tried so often to do things on my own. The myth of independence has let me down, and it will let you down as well. Resisting help will only cause you to stumble. I now understand that we can go much farther when we let those who love us help carry our burdens.

It takes humility to accept help. Humbling yourself can feel humiliating. But in the end, achieving the impossible can only come when you submit to a strength that is greater than yours alone. God will empower you by his Spirit to accomplish the calling he has placed on your life. He will surround you with his people, for there is strength in the community of saints.

Throughout the Scriptures, the Lord instructs his people to love one another by bearing one another's burdens. It would stand to reason that if we're commanded to bear one another's burdens, we should also accept one another's help. It may feel humbling, and even pathetic, to admit that we can't live life on our own. It takes great courage to expose our weakness and ask for help. But accepting help does not mean we are pitifully weak; it means we are wise.

Consider Jesus, who on the way to the cross, about to fulfill his life's ultimate calling—to die for the sins of mankind—was weak on all fronts: emotionally drained by anxiety and dread, spiritually weary from crying out to the Father to be spared from a criminal's death, and physically exhausted from standing trial all night and carrying a solid wooden crossbeam. When Roman soldiers made Simon of Cyrene carry the cross for Jesus, he allowed Simon to bear his burden. Undoubtedly, at that moment Jesus could have utilized the dynamic power of the Spirit who would soon overcome death and raise him from the grave. Instead, he humbled himself and let Simon bear his burden.

Jesus was a unfailing example of what it means to be human and to live a life that is truly full. Let him serve as your example. We can find great encouragement to make it to the end when we allow others to bear our burdens. Reach out and let others lift you up.

Isolation will kill us; community will sustain us.

----

*Accepting help does not mean you're
pitifully weak; it means you are wise.*

----

*I wondered if I had misunderstood God's
calling on my life. I considered quitting.*

----

1. What is a piece of wisdom you have gained by
   accepting help in your life?

2. When things get confusing, what is your compass for
   discerning whether you should continue forward?

CHAPTER 9

Strength to Start

Remember to smile.

NELSON MANDELA

Set your intention.

I learned this axiom when I learned yoga. I learned yoga after I learned I wasn't flexible enough to ride a bike for more than forty miles at a time without having the chemotherapy in my system cause cramping, and my tight hamstrings to strain my back. My chiropractor couldn't solve my problems, and I wondered if my body could survive the 112-mile bike ride. I came to see that my lack of flexibility was my biggest obstacle to finishing IRONMAN.

My old friend Joe Hawley was in town visiting. He had just retired from a career in the NFL. The starting center for the Tampa Bay Buccaneers for eight years, he decided to retire early, before his body and mind were completely battered. He sold all his possessions, bought a Sprinter van, adopted a rescue dog, and traveled around the country. He was on a quest to find purpose for his life "after the game" and healing for his body after countless snaps.[1]

---

1. Joe now leads a network of leaders who infuse their businesses and relationships with

Joe also took up yoga. I asked him to show me some moves he thought might be helpful for me. It's amazing to see a monster of a man who once weighed three hundred pounds extend into a perfect back bridge. He taught me a handful of moves that I include in my morning routine, and these new practices allowed me to gain the necessary mobility for going the full distance on the bike.

But yoga taught me an even more valuable lesson—to set my intention.

IRONMAN Race Day

My alarm went off at 4:00 a.m. on October 9, 2020—race day. My intention had been set: be grateful. Let me share how I arrived at this specific focus. I've never been an "it's all about the journey" kind of guy. I'm definitely not good at the whole "relax and enjoy the ride" thing. Instead, for better or worse, I'm outcome-focused. I've always set goals, not intentions. I set my sights on a goal and try never to waver. The morning of the race, establishing an intention helped me let go of all the things that were out of my control that day and embrace the journey with gratitude, no matter how the day might unfold.

Sometimes the journey of reaching the goal is enjoyable, and sometimes it's not. But I always enjoy the feeling of accomplishment. Until ... I don't. Then I set my sights on a new goal and push through until I reach a new accomplishment. I enjoy that for a bit, and then I hit repeat.

My triathlon coach, Margaret, sensed this and often slipped in a comment as she described my next workout. "It will be hard, but remember, it's supposed to be enjoyable." I trust Margaret, so I took her at her word. I tried my best to enjoy the workouts, and I soon

---

tangible, spiritual values to accelerate the potential of high-impact leadership in a completely new, heart-centered way. For more details, see The Härt Collective website (www.thehartcollective.com).

noticed that the more I acknowledged things I was thankful for during the worst moments, the more I enjoyed the workout—things like, "Wow, I have a training partner today; it's great to have someone to push me." Or, "Okay, I'm training solo today; it'll be great to have some time to myself this morning." And even, "Welp, I just accidentally peed in my supertight Lycra bike shorts and I've got to pedal for another thirty miles . . . this will be a great story to tell Hero when I get home [oh, and I hope I don't chafe!]."[2]

I'm glad my coach gave me that helpful advice. Every morning before training, I prayed and asked God for strength, and then I set my intention for the workout: enjoy the ride.

I left my house in the dark of morning. I drove toward the coast and was mindful of the crazy ride my life was taking me on and the endurance it had already required of me, even before I stood at the starting line. During the fifteen months in my life when I was training every day for IRONMAN, I paid special attention to any Bible passage that had to do with perseverance, endurance, power, and strength. Nehemiah 8:10 stuck out to me: "Don't be dejected and sad, for the joy of the LORD is your strength!" (NLT).

What a simple and significant truth! One of the great benefits of trusting Jesus is that we don't need to be dejected and sad even when we get bad news and are walking a path we never would have chosen for ourselves. This is because God is at work in all things for the good of those who love him and have been called according to his purpose (Romans 8:28). What's more, God offers a supernatural joy that can turn sorrow into strength.

I sat in wonder as I pondered this promise of God. It was 6:00 a.m., and I was seated in the front row at my own IRONMAN opening ceremony at the Newport Dunes Waterfront Resort. At the gazebo overlooking the water, Steve Carter stood before a small crowd in the

---

2. I have made the amazing discovery that you can pee in triathlon shorts, continue to bike for hours, and not chafe!

crisp air, lit up by outdoor event lighting. He gave an inspirational speech, talking about turning opposition into opportunity and making a few jokes at my expense. Steve is a good friend from college. Twenty years ago, we prayed with each other daily. We stood up in each other's weddings. All these years later, he jumped on a plane and stood with me in the ceremony to mark the beginning of a seemingly impossible feat intended to show Hero a grand gesture of love. In the crowd were about seventy-five family members, friends, and congregation members. They had all showed up to support me, cheer me on, and witness the power of God. Their energy was electric, and I was moved to tears by their excitement and support.

As we moved from the seats to the starting line, I heard my people hooting and hollering. My people brought the party. I took my place at the starting line. Although I stood alone, no other athletes beside me, I was far from abandoned. Natalie and Hero were there with me, as they had always been and, I'm convinced, will always be. A chorus of cheers echoed on my behalf. And I thought, *Only in the kingdom of God.*

When a person gets diagnosed with a terminal illness, it's typical that despair will follow, and their loved ones will offer somber words of comfort. But at the IRONMAN starting line, I experienced a taste of the kingdom of God. Instead of retreating and relinquishing my dream of completing IRONMAN for my daughter, I was standing at the precipice of an attempt to achieve something that seemed impossible—especially with a cancer-battered body.

My brothers and sisters arrived by the carload to help carry my burden by ringing cowbells, blowing air horns, and cheering their heads off. Only in the kingdom of God could a devastating diagnosis pave the way for a rapturous celebration. So unusual was this scene that strangers came closer to check it out. When they heard the story—that this guy was attempting IRONMAN in the strength of the Lord in spite of brain cancer—they stayed to witness the miracle and joined in the rejoicing.

I had plenty of reasons to be sad and dejected, but that morning it was clear that the joy of the Lord was my strength.

God's strength carried me through difficult training days and was with me at the starting line. For months, every time my wake-up alarm went off, I prayed that God would give me the strength to complete my training regimen. Then I would put two feet on the ground and trust God for the rest. Without fail, God provided me with the power I needed. That morning was no different.

Your mornings are just like mine. Listen to me: *You need to put two feet on the ground.* (Physically if you can, but at least metaphorically.) It's time to get up. Cry out to God, put both feet on the ground, and trust him to provide the rest. It's scary to start from the bottom. Having to start from the bottom is what stops most people from trying. It's humbling to admit you are at the bottom, and it's terrifying to realize how difficult it is to rise from the position you find yourself in.

Once you find the courage to admit your weakness, you can begin to move beyond what you ever thought was possible. You're weaker than you'd like to admit, but you're stronger than you could ever dream. At the starting line, I stood at the beginning of a test I was likely to fail. I wasn't an endurance athlete. I wasn't even an athlete back in high school. Even if my frail body could make it 140.6 miles, it was doubtful I could do it in less than seventeen hours. But there I was—at the starting line. It wouldn't be about how fast I went; it would be about the courage to go for it at all. And I was going to enjoy that simple fact.

In the short window of time I was staged at the starting line, looking out at the Pacific Ocean at dawn and waiting for the sounding of the horn, I took a deep breath and remembered my intention: be grateful for everything. I was instantly grateful for my support team, and I was grateful to have made it to the starting line.[3]

---

3. A famous saying among IRONMAN triathletes is this: the hardest part of IRONMAN is getting to the starting line.

And I was grateful I wasn't paralyzed. One of the major risks of brain surgeries is paralysis. The surgeon removed portions of my brain in the quadrant that affected movement. When I went into surgery, I didn't know if I'd emerge able to walk. But within a half hour after my surgery, I got out of bed, filmed a YouTube video in which I thanked everyone who had prayed for me, and took a walk around the neurosurgery wing. It was an exhilarating moment.

I came out of a super-high-risk surgery with no debilitating injuries, either physical or cognitive, and that was something to be profoundly grateful for. I knew the next 140 miles of my journey were going to be difficult. The sun hadn't yet risen as the race began, and I'd still be racing long after it set. Despite the grueling test I was going to put my body through, with the difficulty compounded by the effects of cancer treatment, I was genuinely thankful that I could stand at the starting line, ready to swim, bike, and run.

The Starting Line

Standing there, trying to stay loose, I took a deep, cleansing breath. Then my friends started the countdown: "... three, two, one!" Natalie and Hero sounded the horn. The race began. I hit Start on my watch and charged toward the Pacific Ocean. As I dove in, the cold, dark water slapped me in the face and woke me up completely. I felt invigorated. I moved like a man fueled by the Spirit, not like a cancer patient injected with chemotherapy. I swam alongside a footbridge some ten feet off the water, spanning approximately three hundred feet. My friends had run from the starting line and were now spread out along the bridge. They cheered so loudly that I could hear them, even with my head down, ears submerged in the water. Every time I took a breath on my right-hand side, I could see them. Some were leaning over the rail cheering, and some were waving. Two guys had giant "IronDad" flags, which they waved as they ran back and forth on the bridge.

The dawn was beginning to break, and there was just enough

light to be able to make out individual faces. Halfway down the bridge, I saw Natalie and Hero. For just an instant, I locked eyes with my daughter. She felt the connection and waved at me. I was at a point in my stroke that my hand was out of the water at its highest peak, so I waved back! Hero started to jump for joy and squeal. Seeing her so happy and feeling so connected with her filled my heart with joy.[4]

I started kicking harder and pulling faster, and I was propelled forward with joy. My soul learned that the joy of the Lord truly is my strength. I had read this truth in Nehemiah 8:10, but at that moment I fully experienced it for the first time.

When you set your intention to be grateful, this joy is available for you to experience too.

The Doorway to Joy

About a mile into the swim, I found my rhythm. *Kick, pull, breathe. Kick, pull, breathe.* My pace was faster than I expected, but I didn't feel taxed. I slipped into a meditative state as I glided through the vast sea. I slowly worked through the Lord's Prayer. I relished the scene at the starting line as I prayed, "Your kingdom come, your will be done, on earth as it is in heaven." Then when I reached the portion of the prayer asking for daily bread, I repeatedly requested that God's strength would be granted to me.

As I meditated on this petition, the Holy Spirit connected some dots for me. The doorway to the Almighty's storehouse of strength was his joy. And the key to unlocking the joy of the Lord was gratitude. By obeying the command of 1 Thessalonians 5:18 ("give thanks in all circumstances") I would be able to open the door to joy and access God's supernatural strength.

---

4. I later asked Hero about this moment. She said she had dropped her stick into the water and got excited because she thought I'd be able to get it back for her! Hahaha—kids!

All those who peer through that open door will see a picture of God's kingdom unlike anything they've seen on this earth. My story is of someone who should have felt cursed, but instead I felt blessed. I should have felt sad, but I rejoiced. I should have been too weak to race 140.6 miles in less than seventeen hours, but I had enough courage to try.

I continued swimming and continued communing with the Spirit. I thought about 1 Thessalonians 5:18, and Jesus reminded me of what Pastor Kyle Zimmerman of Friends Church in Orange had pointed out in a sermon: 1 Thessalonians commands us to be thankful *in* all circumstances, not *for* all circumstances. Making the distinction between these two small prepositions makes a big difference. I do not give thanks *for* my cancer diagnosis; but I am thankful even *in* my fight with cancer.

Big difference!

—

Months before, a man and his wife came up to me after learning I had terminal brain cancer. They told me that the man had the same type of tumor I did and that having cancer was the best thing that had ever happened to him.

I appreciated their attempt to encourage me, but I wasn't buying it. They were trying to be obedient to 1 Thessalonians 5:18, I suppose, but their comment revealed that they were trying to be thankful *for* something terrible. I had no doubt that they had experienced many good things since his battle began. And many of those blessings may well have been a direct result of his disease. A lot of people reorder their priorities when they can no longer deny that their days are numbered. And that is fantastic.

But as I talked further with this couple, I could tell that his surgeries had resulted in some brain damage and that his body was suffering from years of treatment. His life had extended well beyond the prognosis he had been given—which surely can be seen as a miracle. However, his quality of life had significantly declined, and it seemed quite clear that every year was a struggle.

Sometimes my religiosity tempts me to feign gratitude for the evil disease I've been afflicted with. But Jesus has taught me that I don't have to pretend to not see the misfortune of my life while holding on to a righteous and positive perspective. Instead, he gives me courage to face disappointment and still find legitimate reasons to be thankful *in* my difficult circumstances. Believe me, if I were going to attempt IRONMAN to teach my daughter to boldly go after the dreams God has placed in her heart, and I was given a choice to do the race with or without cancer, I would definitely choose the *sans cancer* option! Not only would it mean that chemotherapy would not be suppressing my white blood cell count and restricting the oxygen flow to my muscles (a vital component for any endurance athlete), but it would also mean I would not only inspire my daughter to go after her dreams, but I would have a greater likelihood of being present to see her achieve them.

No, I will not pretend to be thankful *for* a terminal illness that, given the odds, will likely cut short my life span. But I will practice the powerful discipline of giving thanks *in light of my illness*. I will not back down, retreat, and give up. Instead, I will identify God's very real presence in my time of trouble, acknowledge the blessings he provides each day, and lean on his strength to keep going. I will stay strong and press on to the very end.

You, too, my friend, have access to supernatural strength to stay strong and press on. God's joy is your strength. God's powerful joy comes by exercising gratitude in every situation in which you find yourself. Practice gratefulness daily, and in your day of need, you will find strength fueled by joy. You will be empowered to rise up, push through, and overcome adversity.

Immeasurably More

After swimming about two miles, I still felt good. Many people had told me they had attempted IRONMAN multiple times but couldn't complete the swim in the two hours and twenty minutes allotted. At this point, it was clear that God heard my prayer and was giving me strength to finish the swim portion of the race before the cutoff time. I was grateful that he granted me my wish, but then he surprised me.

One of my favorite Bible verses declares that God "is able to do immeasurably more than all we ask or imagine, according to his power that is at work within us" (Ephesians 3:20). With less than a half mile to swim, I received from God a different kind of strength—a strength I didn't even know I needed to ask for. He gave me the strength to forgive. It came out of nowhere. I was swimming and communing with God, and suddenly my mind turned to deep emotional pain from long ago.

After becoming a Christian and learning that God calls us to forgive just as Christ has forgiven us, I committed to be a forgiving person. But I soon learned that forgiving is easier said than done. As I attempted to forgive people from my past, I found that I could mentally assent to forgiveness of the big grievances, but it was harder to dig deep into my soul and forgive from my heart.

I had worked with mentors and therapists to forgive the best I could. For the most part, I was satisfied with my emotional progress and felt free, as the old saying goes, from drinking the poison of bitterness and hoping others will die. I had made peace with the fact that past pain continues to show up in current relationships, and I knew I'd have to keep learning techniques to create different relationships from ones in my past.

But as I swam along on that early morning, a chain broke free. I won't name the person or describe the events, but I will say I had been haunted and held back by my past. I can't tell you how it happened. It wasn't something logical or mechanical as I had tried before. Something deep inside of me broke free, similar to what I felt coming out of my first brain surgery. I can only attribute it to God's presence.

Reflecting on that moment reminds me of how the Bible begins:

In the beginning God created the heavens and the earth. Now the earth was formless and empty, darkness was over the surface of the deep, and the Spirit of God was hovering over the waters.
(GENESIS 1:1–2)

It's a story describing a good God who entered chaos and created beauty from nothing. Here I was, swimming through the waters of a dark abyss, and God was present, hovering. As the light began to break forth, God began his work—strengthening me for the task and working deeper and deeper, creating beauty out of a dark past. After 2.4 miles of swimming, I emerged from the saltwater and felt like I had just received a new baptism. I was changed. Instead of my strength being taxed, I felt like I was given fresh strength that would carry me on step-by-step.

I transitioned onto my bike and headed for the Pacific Coast Highway. The sun was rising and painting the sky with all of the beautiful colors that California is known for. I felt so grateful that competing alone allowed me to ride the PCH. It is a famous ride for cyclists. People fly in from all over to ride this route. And it was a perfect day for riding: temperatures in the low 70s, no headwinds, and beautiful scenery.

Although I wasn't surrounded by any other competing athletes, I did have an entourage with me. A chase vehicle rode behind me with a paramedic to keep me safe, a bike tech because I still didn't know much about bikes, and a professional photographer for posterity's sake. Next to me were two camera crews filming the event—one crew with IRONMAN staff broadcasting to their platforms and another crew with a documentarian capturing the whole story. I had an abundance of support.

As I approached the first major intersection, two motorcycle police officers pulled up next to me and slowed down to my speed. *Uh-oh. I had a chase van behind me and two camera crews next to me. Were we supposed to get a permit for this?* More than just a hiccup, this could be a major problem. They put on their lights. And then instead of pulling me over, both officers sped ahead! They entered the intersection ahead of me and stopped traffic so I could blow through. Then they caught up to me again and closed down the next intersection.

I had a police escort on the entire course. A friend from church—a retired police lieutenant—had coordinated with multiple police departments in multiple cities to arrange the escort for me. So much fun!

I felt like a pro riding the Tour de France. I wasn't going nearly as fast as those guys, but whatever. It was really, really fun. Best ride ever. I was full of joy and gratitude. Under these circumstances, the ride went relatively quickly and wasn't too taxing at all. I felt great.

Strength in Joy and Sadness

Trust me, not every ride has felt great. Joy has not always fueled my cycling. In fact, I've cried a lot while out on rides.

Does that make you feel uncomfortable? If it does, hang with me for a few sentences. When you read about a man crying, what does it stir up in you? I didn't cry when I received my diagnosis or prognosis—terminal brain cancer and a life cut short. Not a tear. I felt deep pain in my heart every time I thought about leaving my family early. Sometimes my eyes would get glassy and my voice would even crack, but I would always stop short. Why? I don't know. Maybe I grew up in a culture where real men don't cry. Men are strong and tears are weak. Or maybe building walls to keep deep emotions out was my way of protecting myself from feelings I didn't want to experience. I just don't know.

But what I do know is that for me, tears didn't come easy or often. But out on the bike, cycling in solitude for four or five hours at a time, something extraordinary would sometimes happen. Tears.

I have an idea why. I think it's possible that the rhythmic, circular motion of legs pedaling has the power to unlock emotion. And after a few hundred thousand revolutions and being left alone in your thoughts, something breaks free. It all felt very similar to the EMDR treatments I did after my dad died. EMDR (eye movement desensitization and reprocessing) is a therapeutic technique that was developed to help war veterans heal from posttraumatic stress disorder. Psychologists found that it worked for anyone who had experienced trauma. My childhood experience of suddenly losing my dad caused a certain level of trauma—enough to affect me significantly every time I entered a hospital, which I did often as a pastor.

After I became frustrated with my inability to minister well to hurting church members in the hospital setting, I sought out EMDR treatment. And it worked. The results after just a few sessions were huge. And I believe I experienced something similar while cycling. Much like EMDR, the rhythmic movement of the bike and my legs helped heal the trauma of being diagnosed with a terminal illness.[5]

The physical strength needed to take on an IRONMAN competition while battling cancer is enormous. But it's also important to focus on the emotional strength that's needed to overcome such a challenge. A lot of guys experience internal strife but are resistant to therapy. I've been there. I know what it's like to think I can make it on my own.

I now know, though, that life is better if you work on building inner strength as well as physical strength. I needed a good coach to prepare for IRONMAN. I also needed a good therapist to help me gain deep, meaningful connections with my wife and my daughter.

---

5. Full disclosure: I'm still in therapy, but cycling gave me a good start.

It's not easy, but you can do hard things. If you're the tough guy, it's time to stop being afraid. Get into counseling.

———

I had just swum 2.4 miles and cycled 112. As I pulled into the transition zone for the run, I felt great.

For the first 115 miles, I felt superhuman. Powered by gratitude and persevering on joy, I found myself two hours ahead of my planned pace and four hours ahead of the cutoff time. I had been smiling for miles and was surprised by how good my body felt. I was amazed at how much energy I still had in the bank.

I started my run with the plan of running nine-minute miles. That's a slow pace compared to the pros, but compared to those doing IRONMAN for the first time or even racing their first marathon, it was a respectable speed. Because I had just gone 115 miles and still had a full marathon to go, I started my run at a relaxed pace, an estimated nine and a half minutes per mile. After a half mile, I looked at my watch . . . and I was running at an eight-minute-mile pace! *Slow down!* I told myself. *It's not a sprint; it's a marathon—literally.*

At the one-mile mark, my watch buzzed, and I expected to see one mile at the ten-minute mark. But I had completed the first mile of the marathon in eight and a half minutes. My legs and lungs were telling me I could go all day at this pace. I considered cautiously remaining at this pace for a while longer. I thanked God for lending me his strength and allowing me to feel so energized this deep into the race.

And then something disastrous happened. I burped. But it was more than that; it was my stomach's way of telling me it was mad at me.

*It wasn't about succeeding or failing; it was
about actually going for it at all.*

1. Is fear of failure a limiting factor in a certain area of
   your life?

You need to put two feet on the ground.

*God's powerful joy comes by exercising gratitude
in every situation you find yourself.*

2. What do you need to begin doing that you keep
   putting off?

3. What does the word *joy* bring up in you as you
   think about it? Is it the same as happiness? Do you
   consider yourself a joyful person? Why or why not?
   Does joy depend on anything? If so, on what?

CHAPTER 10

Feeling Strong . . . Until I Wasn't

It's not that bad.[1]

JEREMIAH COX

Going into the race, I knew that my cancer treatment was going to create an obstacle that I'd need to overcome. But I wasn't sure what that meant in practical terms. Seizure was my main concern. Overexerting myself had previously led to having a seizure, and if it happened on race day, it would end my race. Because of the cramping I experienced during training, I figured I'd have to battle that also at some point during the race. To avoid cramping I focused on sticking to my nutrition and hydration plan. What I didn't count on was the fact that chemotherapy had wreaked havoc on my digestive system, and, yes, that complicated things.

Although I had done well in eating and drinking throughout the miles, my stomach didn't do such a great job of digesting the goos,

---

1. This was something my friend said to me as we backpacked through Europe while I was in college.

gels, bars, and electrolytes. Over the past nine hours, I had put a *lot* into my stomach, and it was all just sitting there. I wasn't absorbing any of the nutrients or water through my gut lining. As a result, everything was accumulating in my stomach until there was no more room in the inn. Everything in me wanted to come out. I went from feeling like I could run endlessly to feeling the impossibility of the task ahead. After racing 116 miles, I still had to run a marathon while feeling like I had the stomach flu.

I prayed the same thing you would have prayed: *God, help.* Simple yet effective. Up to this point, the storehouse of gratitude I had built up kept me positive. But now, instead of being grateful for nice things—like the view of the Pacific Ocean while cycling up the Pacific Coast Highway and for the police escort that shut down intersections, allowing me to blow through red lights—I was feeling grateful for past difficulties. I had felt sick to my stomach before and had still accomplished physical activities. I was grateful for all the days I had to push through the feelings of nausea from chemo while training.

I was thankful for the time, years ago, when I climbed Mount Whitney with friends too quickly and got hit hard with altitude sickness at the peak. We had quickly climbed to fifteen thousand feet and made it to the top in five hours. Without acclimating, I became very dizzy and nauseous, and the climb down passageways, with sheer cliffs covered in ice, required a much slower pace. Every minute was excruciating.

As I ran the last leg of IRONMAN, I reflected on that experience and thought to myself, *Well, what I am feeling now isn't as bad as what I felt like on Mount Whitney. I had no choice but to keep moving on the mountain. And I did it. I did it then, and I can do it again.* And then and there I developed a new mantra: *It's not that bad.*

Jeremiah Cox, one of my good friends, introduced me to this mantra when I was nineteen years old. We were in college and doing the classic coming-of-age ritual—backpacking through Europe. Five of us guys scraped together just enough money for plane tickets, a Eurail Pass, and just a few more bucks for a daily meal or two and a bed at a hostel.

Every day, we stood in a new breathtaking location, checking off all the must-see experiences in Europe. Some nights we shared a hostel room with other broke young travelers who smelled equally as horrid. Some nights we slept on the floor of locals we had met and convinced to let us in. Some nights we slept on the grass in parks.

We were taking in high culture, although not participating in it. We saw the *Mona Lisa*, but we were hangry after not eating much that day.[2] We stood atop the Eiffel Tower, but we hiked up the stairs because we didn't have enough money for the elevator. We went to the Colosseum, but only half of us had enough cash to pay to go inside and imagine what it felt like to be a gladiator on the stadium floor.[3] We ran with the bulls in Pamplona, but we didn't rent an apartment above the route like John Hemingway did; instead, we stayed up all night.

When I list it out, it seems like a lot of fun. And it was, but we encountered difficulties as well. Anytime one of the guys started to get grumpy or complain, Jeremiah would start to chant, "It's not that bad. It's not that bad." It was super awkward to be the loud Americans chanting in public, but we would all join in. When we were irritable, the chanting was super annoying. But eventually it would snap us out of it and we'd laugh and enjoy whatever was awaiting us.

One day while in Hallstatt, Austria, we hiked along a river up the most amazing hillside. It felt like we had escaped civilization and found a secret paradise. At one point, we had to scramble up some rocks. We reached the plateau, where the river turned into a small lake, maybe a hundred feet in diameter. The water was crystal clear and glowed blue and green from the minerals on the rock walls

---

2. As an American who thinks bigger is better, I was disappointed by how small the *Mona Lisa* is.
3. I didn't have enough money to go inside.

below the water. On the other side of the small lake, we could see a cave only about ten feet below the water level. Twenty feet above the cave, a waterfall was pounding down from a cliff, disappearing behind a rock formation. We discovered that the waterfall had made a twenty-foot hole that became the cave that fed the lake. It looked like we'd be able to swim across the lake, down and through the cave, and stand at the bottom of the hole, where the waterfall would swirl around us—and that was what we set out to do.

We didn't expect the water to be so cold, though it should have occurred to us that the snowcapped mountains fed the river that created the lake, filling it with ice-cold water. The first guy stripped and charged at the lake. He jumped in and instantly started screaming. The cold water took his breath away. He got out of the water as fast as possible. We all jumped in, and we all screamed, flailed, and failed. Naked and freezing, we stood at the edge of the lake, trying to figure out a way to make it through the cave. And then (I promise this is true) two middle-aged local women, who were out for a hike and heard us screaming, came around the corner, snapped a quick candid photo of the five nude Americans, and walked away without saying a word.

Jeremiah started chanting, "It's not that bad." We laughed and joined in. *It's not that bad! It's not that bad!* Then one of the guys charged at the lake again, but instead of jumping feetfirst, he dove headfirst deep into the water and kicked hard. Without coming up for a breath, he swam through the underwater cave and stood in the fresh air, with the waterfall swirling around him. And so, with our mantra on our lips, we all made it.

And now, with twenty-five miles left in the race, I started to quietly chant to myself, *It's not that bad.*

Strength in the Attempt

I kept going. I thought about Mount Whitney. I thought about difficult training days. I thought about my second brain surgery. The unforgettable memories from the second surgery both traumatized me and empowered me. I strongly remember the searing pain of having my inflamed scalp stapled back together as my skull was held motionless by a metal clamp. I also strongly remember the resolve I had when I told the surgeon to proceed despite the pain. The experience felt terrible, but I did it.

I felt that same way as I ran. On the one hand, compared to the 120 miles I had already gone, twenty miles is not very far. On the other hand, twenty miles is a long run. And when you've already done 120 miles, adding another twenty miles while feeling sick seems impossible.

In the moment, I desperately wanted to complete the race without delay. The memories of my second surgery gave me the courage to keep going. At the 120-mile mark, I was thankful for the past difficulties I had already made it through. Romans 5:3–5 (NLT) was playing out in real time in my life:

> We can rejoice, too, when we run into problems and trials, for we know that they help us develop endurance. And endurance develops strength of character, and character strengthens our confident hope of salvation. And this hope will not lead to disappointment. For we know how dearly God loves us, because he has given us the Holy Spirit to fill our hearts with his love.

For the next ten miles of the run, I was mentally locked in. I kept pushing through the pain and nausea. Feeling the fatigue of my body, my mind finally acknowledged what I was too afraid to confront: if during the previous 130 miles I couldn't absorb the vital nutrients and hydration, I wasn't going to make it. I was going to cramp. Even professional triathletes cramp up on this race.[4] My chemo-filled body wasn't going to be able to go the distance with

---

4. IRONMAN has a highlight film of athletes cramping and crawling over the finish line.

no fuel. No matter how resolved I was, if my body cramped up miles from the finish line, my day would be done.

I had to make peace with this. I knew that God's grace would prove sufficient. Mercifully in that moment of reckoning, God's Spirit met me and whispered an encouragement I never would have come up with on my own: *There is strength in the attempt.*

I decided right then and there that even if Hero wouldn't see me cross the finish line, I was going to look her in the eye and tell her I gave it my all to make it home to her. Someday I may have to say this to her regarding my battle with cancer. I was resolved in my heart to keep going until I couldn't go any farther and to count the hundred-plus miles not as a failure, but as a strong attempt. I changed my mantra once again. With the rhythm of my breathing, I repeated to myself, *You have nothing to prove, just an example to set. You have nothing to prove, just an example to set.*

At this point on the course, I passed by my church's aid station. Nancy Foster, a spiritual mother of mine, was there. Although I never asked her, I can guarantee you she saw me and prayed for me. Val Selvig was there too. I had gotten to know Val when her kids came through the youth group. She's a prayer warrior, and I know she prayed for me too. While I heard her say something to me, I can't remember exactly what she said, but I do recall that she called me "Honey," which felt comforting in my soul. My body, however, was so weak I didn't even reply. I felt like I was being rude. I just kept running.

As the sun began to set, I saw the next aid station and saw my coach, Margaret. She had gotten word that I was sick and tracked me down. As I ran like a zombie by the aid station, she joined me and ran alongside me. She kept me going.

How great it is to have someone beside you! The proverbs writer had it right: "As iron sharpens iron, so one person sharpens another" (Proverbs 27:17). As we ran, Margaret helped me troubleshoot. Then she pulled out a vial of salt. I had too many electrolytes in my stomach and not enough in my blood, and sodium helps balance it. She told me to place the salt under my tongue to get it into my bloodstream faster. At mile 135, I started to feel better. I started drinking water again. I had a chance of finishing.

My coach saved my race. The love of God filled my heart. I pressed on toward home.

Flexibility Is Strength

Resilience is often thought of as the strength to endure, a grit that never quits, the unbreakable determination of an iron will. All of that is true to an extent. But we must also remember the truth that to be resilient is to be flexible or malleable, to be able to absorb, adapt, and recover. Perfectionists see an ideal ending and can't see the opportunities present when a change in course is needed. They can't even imagine a different way. I am a perfectionist. If you are as well, then resilience becomes difficult to achieve. Resilience requires flexibility.

Just as a building must flex in order to withstand an earthquake, we must flex to be able to persist through the difficulties of life. You may start your day with a particular intention. However, you are not in control of how any day may unfold, so you must be willing to change your intention as needed. You are not in control. Fortunately, you serve a God who is, a God whose grace is sufficient and whose power is made perfect in weakness. He delights in offering you his strength. Trust him. Let go and make the necessary adjustments, even if doing so doesn't seem ideal. He will give you the power to fight the good fight, the strength to finish the race, and the resilience to keep the faith.

The only way to become more flexible is through regular stretching. Here are two ways to mentally and emotionally stretch yourself on your journey to resilience:

1. **Ask for advice and accept it.** I'm not asking you to take

advice from just anyone on situations that have a major impact on your life. Instead, I'm suggesting that you ask for advice in the more benign areas of life. In situations you routinely encounter, ask someone who has been successful in facing these challenges how they approached them. Then apply their approach to your task. See things from their perspective and develop your own perspective. Not only do you have a chance to improve your skill set, but you can also build a larger toolbox for those times when unexpected changes arise.

2. **Get out of your comfort zone and learn something new.** Engaging calculated risks that require skills and knowledge you don't yet have will take you out of your comfort zone and stretch your resilience. Learning new skills will reinforce your confidence that you can learn to do important things to problem-solve the difficulties of life. Developing a growth mindset will stretch your thinking and create more flexibility and resilience.

Without flexibility, you can snap. All strength and no flexibility are stubbornness and perfectionism. Keep stretching yourself so you can experience the strength of flexibility. Resilient living requires a staunch ability to absorb, adapt, and flex. If you can flex, you can continue.

140.6

The sun had set.

I was almost there. But yet there was still a long way to go.

It's a strange feeling to start racing in the dark, race all day, and continue racing into the dark again. I was now in my hometown, but I felt a long way from home. I was five miles from the finish line. I ran at an exhausted pace. I pressed on through the night toward the finish. Out of nowhere, a squad car began to follow me, its headlights lighting the way for me. My friend Pat Thayer, who had arranged the police escort at the beginning of the race, had planned to have another escort for the end.

When I was just a couple miles from my house, the officers started the preparty. With their lights flashing, they played AC/DC over the loudspeaker.[5] They called for backup. Two cars showed up, and then two more. I laughed out loud when I realized that I was a pastor running from the cops.

Then they began encouraging me over the loudspeaker: "You've got this. We're with you. Keep going. We're proud of you. You're gonna do this." Man, I never expected that. The lights, the music, their encouragement—all of it put fresh breath in my lungs and lightened my step. One of the Latin words for *encourage* is *animo*, which paints the word picture of animating an object by filling it with breath and making it come alive, freshly emboldened. There is power when your community is surrounding you, encouraging you, and supporting you.

Finally, after thirteen hours of racing, I turned into my neighborhood. In the distance I could see the lights glowing in front of my house and I could hear the celebration that awaited me at the finish line. As I got closer, illuminated now by the five Placentia PD cars following me, my friend Kevin spotted me, and I heard his one-of-a-kind laughter. Joy fueled me down the homestretch. I turned onto my street. I ran through a passageway of support, loved ones on both sides falling in behind me and running me home. I looked at the huge finish tower in front of my house, with the IRONMAN finish tape stretched out across the street, and there they were—I saw Natalie and Hero. Together they waited at the finish line, holding a sign that read, THERE'S NO PLACE LIKE THE FINISH LINE. Everyone and everything else faded into a blur except for these two beautiful

---

5. Can you imagine the big grin on my face?

people. Love lifted me. I floated on air to them and crossed the finish line. I still can't believe I did it!

"Jay Hewitt, you are an IRONMAN," blared the public address speakers. Margaret placed the IRONMAN medal around my neck, and I held the finishing tape high over my head.

Every emotion poured over me at once.

Reunited with my family, I kissed Natalie and gave her a bouquet of flowers.

Then I finished what I set out to do. Overcome with hope realized, I turned to Hero and got down on my knee. "If I can do it, you can do it," I told her. I looked her in the eyes and through my tears encouraged her for the future: "Go after the dreams God places in your heart. Don't give up. When life knocks you down, hold on to the hope of Jesus. Find strength in his Spirit. Never give up. Get up, stay strong, and press on. You can do the impossible with God."

I hope that in my weakness she saw God's power demonstrated through me. I hope I set an example for her of resilient faith. When she looks back on this time of life, I hope, more than anything, that she knows I deeply love her, that there is no distance I won't travel for her.

If I can do it, she can do it.

A New Kind of Family

I didn't start life with a great support system, but I have one now. Natalie was there for me when I got the worst news of my life. She had to make complicated career adjustments to be there for me during my two surgeries. Natalie found ways to make recovery as enjoyable as possible. She relocated her life to a different state for more than a month so I could receive the best radiation treatment available. And she gave me the green light to be gone countless hours as I trained for IRONMAN, even as it placed a tremendous amount of stress on her and our family. Hero gave me motivation and courage to strive to be strong in the reality of my weakness.

Let me tell you about some of the other amazing things people did for me. The Fosters were willing to supply a million dollars to cover a surgery that insurance would not. They stepped in as parents because mine were gone. They brought me into their family even before this health challenge began. But now there is no doubt that they care for me as one of their own.

The Hustons organized multiple meal trains and organized friends to visit us in Texas during radiation treatments. My dear friend Joosung Kwon relocated from London (with the sacrificial blessing of his wife, Ime) to capture the entire journey on film so Hero can reflect on this experience later in life. He put his heart and soul into the film as a gift for my family and the rest of the world. He lived with my family for months, and in the process he became family.

Kane followed me the entire race as my own personal paramedic just in case something went wrong. Eric rode with me, and Jimmy ran with me and kept me company during that lonely, virtual race. Brittany tackled the logistics of the race and organized the volunteers—two hundred church members strong. My longtime friend and honorary older-brother figure Jon built the finishing structure. My coach Margaret saved my race. The team from the IRONMAN Foundation made it possible for me to compete in an official 140.6-mile IRONMAN triathlon.

Many more people supported me, but my point is that no one can reach their potential without people who are willing to go the distance with them. I was afraid that those who were there for me at the beginning would suffer from support fatigue and wouldn't be there with me in the end. Happily, I am amazed at the endurance and resilience of their love for me. I set out to show Hero how much I love her. At the end of this endeavor, I was convinced that a multitude of people fiercely love my entire family and will always be there for us.

Do you have people like that in your life? Cultivate relationships now by lifting up those around you, and they will carry you when you need them. We can go a lot farther when we bear one another's burdens. We can't complete the marathon of faith without the strength of the community of saints.

A life well lived is not lived alone.

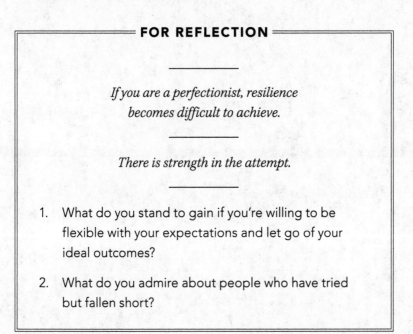

FOR REFLECTION

If you are a perfectionist, resilience becomes difficult to achieve.

There is strength in the attempt.

1. What do you stand to gain if you're willing to be flexible with your expectations and let go of your ideal outcomes?

2. What do you admire about people who have tried but fallen short?

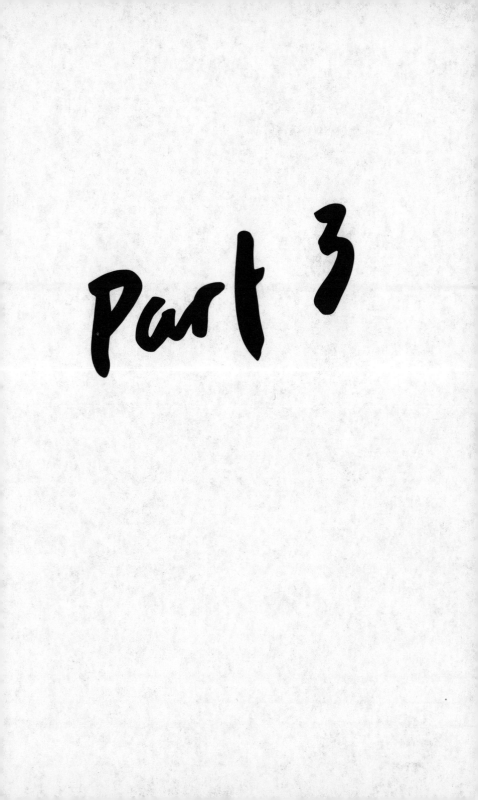

Part 3

CHAPTER 11

How to Do It

*Do what you can, with what
you've got, where you are.*

THEODORE ROOSEVELT

It takes resilient faith to build a resilient life. But how do we
build that kind of faith?

We're going to take a close look at 2 Corinthians 12:9–10 and
unlock Scripture's secrets on how it can be that when we are weak,
we are actually strong. Then we'll reflect on how to find the confidence and motivation needed to access resilience and achieve
victory in life's most difficult moments. We will get extremely practical. I even included a Venn diagram and a flowchart (and a Greek
word study). You're welcome.

If you had been at the finish line with me and we had chatted for
a moment, I would have told you the same thing I told my daughter:
If I can do it, you can do it. Your ability to overcome is not dependent
on your capabilities, but rather on your willingness to admit your
weakness and rely on God to demonstrate his power through you
and bring into sharper focus the strength within you.

I didn't compete in and complete IRONMAN because I am a

uniquely strong person or a natural athlete. I actually wasn't coordinated enough to do a jumping jack until I was twelve years old, and I never played varsity sports in high school. I won't even tell you how much I can bench-press—it's nothing to brag about, and that, my friends, is why I brag about it. An ancient way of faith taught me that it's best to boast in my weakness because it is then that God's power is seen. The Lord is my strength, and I receive his strength through the gift of his Holy Spirit, which was given to me when I put my faith in Jesus. I do not have an iron will, but I do have the strength of the Spirit.

First Things First

Second Corinthians 12:10 has become a profoundly relevant Scripture in my life. The more I meditate on it, the more I recognize some deep details that many people miss when they read the last nine words of the verse:

For when I am weak, then I am strong.

Simple. But here's what I've noticed. Two words make all the difference. We tend to be so focused on the key words *weak* and *strong* that we overlook *when* and *then*.

When I am *weak*, then I am *strong*.

When I am weak, *then* I am strong.

We don't just overlook these words; we replace them with words that aren't even there. We delete *when* and replace *then I am* with the phrase *but God is*.

~~When~~ I am weak, ~~then~~ I am strong.

I am weak, *but God is* strong.

Yes, God is strong, absolutely, but the apostle Paul here in 2 Corinthians didn't say, "I am weak, *but God is strong.*" Even though this statement of comparison is true, it wasn't what Paul was saying.

I also want to point out that Paul wasn't saying, "I am weak *and* I am strong."

~~When~~ I am weak, ~~then~~ I am strong.

I am weak *and* I am strong.

Second Corinthians 12:10 is not a paradoxical statement that said two things can be true at the same time. Paul was making a statement of causality: **when** I am weak, **then** I am strong. If we want to become strong when we're not, we need to understand why Scripture uses these two words. First comes weakness, then strength. Only when we are keenly aware of our weakness can we clearly see that any strength displayed in our lives is clearly not of ourselves but can only be credited to a source beyond us—our God who displays his power in our weakness. When we are merely tired, we may be able to dig deep and find the willpower to move ourselves forward. But when we are truly weak and powerless, then God's Spirit shows up and causes us to be truly strong. God's power working in us is most apparent when we are powerless. **When** we are weak, **then** we are strong.

How to Be a Strong Fighter

Scripture shows us that we can't pretend our way to being strong. We can't fake it till we make it. Becoming strong takes work—uncomfortable work. The first step to becoming strong is admitting you are weak. Admitting your weaknesses isn't easy. For me, feeling weak is the worst feeling. I can barely tolerate feeling needy, fragile, humiliated, frozen, afraid, anxious, insecure, out of control, or powerless. But until you admit you are weak, you will remain weak. You will have an Achilles' heel that will be exploited and at some point you will fall powerless.

This goes against just about everything that culture has taught men in particular about strength and masculinity. But Jesus is countercultural and his strength is true strength. When you admit there are areas where you are weak, vulnerable, incompetent, and even powerless, then you start becoming strong. There can't be strength without vulnerability. But *when* you get vulnerable, *then* you get strong. *When* you are weak, *then* you are strong.

Let me give you an example of how this works. I've mentioned how much I like the sport of boxing. No other sport so clearly demonstrates that it takes the weakness of vulnerability to accomplish something that takes strength. A fighter can't knock out their opponent without making themselves vulnerable to being knocked out themselves. Even in moments when their opponent is hurt and barely staying on their feet, when a fighter loads up and tries to fire a knockout punch, they inevitably open themselves up in some area and become vulnerable to a counterpunch. All too often, right at the time when a fighter is about to knock out their opponent, they get shocked by a punch they didn't see coming and go down for the count. A weak fighter doesn't know they are even vulnerable. Or if they do know, they're too afraid to put themselves in a position that makes themselves vulnerable enough to land a knockout shot. A strong fighter understands their vulnerabilities and is willing to open up their weakness to access the strength needed to win. We must drop the tough-guy facade if we want to become strong.

Now, let me give you an example of how this insight has worked in my own life. Brain cancer left me too weak to lead my church. Yes, it takes more strength to lead a church than to complete IRONMAN. Getting up and going into work is manageable, but the spiritual burden of caring for a congregation is too heavy for me. After finishing IRONMAN, I admitted my weakness and limitations and stepped down from my role as pastor of the church I was leading. I had founded the church, and it was hard to let it go. What happened next astonished me.

When I became too *weak* to continue to lead my church, *then* God gave me the *strongest* ministry of my life. God made me a storyteller. Now he has given me a story to tell. Ever since I was a kid, I've been a good storyteller. Now I have a story to tell about God's grace and power on display in my life—a story that can give people hope and bring glory to God. Whenever I speak from a new stage, I visibly see people find hope in their hardships, the inspiration to create grand gestures of love and faith to turn to Christ and trust him to pull them through the pain. I hope you are experiencing the same as you read this book—my testimony of how God keeps his promise: *when I am weak, then I am strong.* It was hard to admit how weak I was. I'm glad I did.

You must admit you are weak and even dare to open yourself up to that weakness. Then, and only then, will you be positioned to do something requiring great strength. Becoming vulnerable takes strength and produces strength. When you are weak, then you are strong.

Divine Empowerment

But [the Lord] said to me, "My grace is sufficient for you, for my power is made perfect in weakness." Therefore I will boast all the more gladly about my weaknesses, so that Christ's power may rest on me. That is why, for Christ's sake, I delight in weaknesses, in insults, in hardships, in persecutions, in difficulties. For when I am weak, then I am strong. **(2 CORINTHIANS 12:9–10)**

Understanding these two verses of Scripture is crucial for gaining access to a resilient faith and a resilient life. The apostle Paul's words provide a profoundly valuable insight: admitting the weakness of our humanity opens us up to divine empowerment. In verse 9, Jesus declared, "My power is made perfect in weakness." Upon hearing Jesus say this, Paul comes to the conclusion, "When I am weak, then I am strong." The Greek word Jesus used for power is *dynamis*—the same root word Paul used to describe his strength (*dynatos*) that linked with his weakness. Paul is showing that Jesus' power transforms our weakness to strength.

> "My grace is sufficient for you, for my power
> [*dynamis*] is made perfect in weakness."
> "For when I am weak, then I am strong [*dynatos*]."

The words *strength* and *power* are found in the New Testament nearly two hundred times, deriving from ten different Greek words. Paul specifically chose *dynatos* here because he wanted to convey not only a sense of physical strength, power, might, and capability to withstand force or exert force, but also strength of soul. *Dynatos* expresses an inward ability to patiently stand firm against trials and hardship while remaining true to one's own virtues and convictions, maintaining faith that with God, anything is possible.

Interestingly, when Jesus said the things that are impossible for man are possible for God (Matthew 19:26), he used the word *dynatos* to articulate God's ability to make possible (*dynata*) the impossible. God is strong enough to do the impossible. He is stronger than you are and is able to do what you could never do. Not only is God powerful enough, but he delights in displaying his power through your weakness. When you turn to him in your weakness, you can trust that he will strengthen you. This is the heart of God.

I know the heart of God, but I cannot pretend to know the ways of God. How will he transform your weakness to strength? I don't know exactly. His work in you can play out in so many ways. But you can be certain of this: God can do the impossible, and he wants you to come to him with the mountainous catastrophes you face.

Jesus tells us that if we ask God in his name to move mountains, God will grant our request (Matthew 17:20). Jesus doesn't specify *how* God will move the mountain. I've found that God sometimes miraculously moves the mountain and causes it to disappear into the sea. I've seen him miraculously remove tumors from the bodies of friends. Sometimes he lends us his power to climb mountains and reach the other side as though the mountain wasn't even there in the first place. And sometimes, as I'm currently experiencing, God uses his *dynamis* to blow a hole right through the center of the mountain, allowing us to pass through and find some gems along the way. No matter how he chooses to move mountains, God is strong enough to accomplish it. If we are willing to admit the weakness of our humanity and turn toward God, we will open ourselves up to the only power able to overcome the impossible situations we face. All things are possible with the divine power of God that turns our weakness to strength.

Jesus Was Weak

If you have placed your faith in Jesus, you have access to the same power, the same Spirit. As the Scriptures declare, the Spirit that God has given us emboldens us with power (2 Timothy 1:7). Our strength comes when we embrace our weakness and claim the power of God's Holy Spirit as our own. The Holy Spirit is absolute—able to do all things, overcome all things.

Look at the power of the Holy Spirit in Jesus. In Gethsemane, Jesus was heading toward the pain of the cross. In the weakness of his flesh, he was hoping for a way out. Jesus bowed with his face to the ground and prayed, "My Father! If it is possible, let this cup of suffering be taken away from me" (Matthew 26:39 NLT). In his weakness, with blood vessels breaking with anguish and sorrow (Luke 22:44), Jesus pleaded that the trial ahead of him would be taken away, that he would be exempted from the call to do the single most significant action in the course of all of history. And then, thanks be to God, the Holy Spirit enabled him to continue in his prayer and declare, "Yet I want your will to be done, not mine."

As Jesus suffered on the cross, abandoned by his friends and mocked by his enemies, the Spirit gave him the power to forgive as he prayed, "Father, forgive them, for they do not know what they are doing" (Luke 23:34).

As darkness spread across the land and Jesus took his last breath, the Spirit began the ultimate battle with death itself. Three days later, the Spirit overcame the great enemy, broke the chains of death, and breathed life into the body of Jesus, and he rose again into life eternal. That same life and that same Spirit are offered as a gift to all who trust Jesus. The Spirit with its resurrecting power is alive in you. There is nothing you can't do in the name of Jesus and the power of the Spirit!

Go after the dreams God places in your heart. Walk worthy of the calling God has placed on your life. When life knocks you down, hold on to the hope of Jesus, find strength in his Spirit, get up, stay strong, and press on. No matter how difficult life may become, don't give up; get up. If I can do it, you can do it because Jesus has done it for you.

Obstacles and Opportunities

What challenges are you facing today? What obstacles are standing in your way? Know this, an opportunity always resides within the obstacle you face. The Bible declares that "in all things God works for the good of those who love him, who have been called according to his purpose" (Romans 8:28). God is with you, working even the worst things for your good. He brings beauty from ashes and turns obstacles into opportunity. His grace is sufficient for you (2 Corinthians 12:9).

I didn't want to walk this path. I never wanted to hear a doctor say my life is likely to be cut short, that the odds are not in my favor—that I wouldn't be around to raise Hero and that Natalie would lose me. I prayed and asked God to spare me. More than anything, I wanted God to heal me of a cancer with no medical cure. And he may do just that. But until then, I will "make the most of every opportunity in these evil days" (Ephesians 5:16 NLT).

By the grace of God, I saw an opportunity in my diagnosis—an opportunity to show my daughter what true faith looks like, that what the Bible says is true. We really are strong when we are weak. With God, anything is possible. My diagnosis provided a way to practice what I preach and let Hero see my trust in God, even when faith is difficult. It opened a door for me to model authentic faith to my daughter. The overwhelming obstacle I faced opened up opportunities and placed a calling on my life.

What about you? When you're facing an impossible situation, what will you do? When life knocks you down, beats you up, and brings raging storms, what will you do? As far as I can tell, only one truly good option exists. Hold on to hope, lean on the strength of the Lord, and make the most of the opportunity given to you. Be brave and stare down the intimidating obstacle you are facing. Stand your ground long enough to see the opportunity hidden within the obstacle. Then act boldly, and you'll discover God's calling in the season of life in which you find yourself.

God will use your life to display beauty to the world that needs to see authentic, enduring faith. In your weakness, God will show the world a true strength born out of faith—a strength that is beyond you, residing deep inside of you; a sufficient grace pulling you through; a resurrecting power displayed in you; a spiritual strength you can stand on; true strength that cultivates resilience.

Don't compare yourself to me and minimize your struggles

by saying, "Well, I don't have terminal cancer." Good! I hope you never have to deal with a diagnosis like that. But I know you are facing something hard. Hard is hard. And by the powerful Spirit of Jesus, you can do hard things. You've done it before, and you made it through the fire. Faith is forged in the fire and strengthened in the struggle. No matter what obstacle you're facing, you can persevere with the strength of Jesus.

Don't hide your weakness; *boast* in it. Don't hide your vulnerability, fragility, humanity; *put it on display* so God's power can be seen by all those watching. Your moment of greatest weakness will be your biggest opportunity to make an impact. If you face your biggest obstacle head-on, you'll find your greatest opportunity to leave your mark of love in the name of Jesus. Face your obstacle. Make the most of your opportunity. Live a life that matters.

Ingredients of Resilience

Do you want to be a resilient person? Of course you do. But how do you become resilient? It won't be easy; nothing worthwhile ever is.

If you want to be resilient, you need to find a clear *calling* on your life and a *confidence* that the calling can be accomplished. If you want to become more resilient, you don't have to wait passively for calling and confidence to appear; you can actively discover your calling and build your confidence.

Discover Your Calling

Your calling is often found in the obstacles you must face. Residing within key obstacles are valuable opportunities. They can be hard to see, so you must prayerfully look deep within the things that seem impossible to overcome. When obstacles and opportunities emerge, you'll hear a calling to something that's worth giving your life to.

I took everything I learned during my trials and created a life-changing Venn diagram that explains how we can persevere and find resilience.[1]

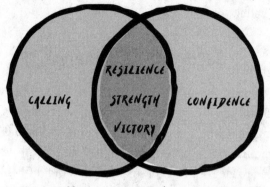

When *calling* and *confidence* collide, you find *resilience*, *strength*, and *victory*.

In my case I saw a calling to something worth dedicating my life to—namely, developing my daughter's faith through my love for her and my trust in God.

Obstacles will not stop you from grabbing hold of opportunities; obstacles will create opportunities. The bigger the obstacle, the greater the opportunity. Examine your weakness and let it become your strength. Give to the world what you wished would have been given to you in your time of need. As the saying goes, let your misery become your ministry. Whatever is about to sink you, flip it on its head and let it lift you to new heights. If you want to soar, you've got to jump off.

Refuse to let obstacles stop you, but rather let them launch you. When obstacles appear—and they will—opportunities will eventually emerge if you just hang on. Don't turn and run from the obstacle; instead, look it straight in the eye and see the opportunity hidden

1. I'm a big believer in the power of a Venn diagram.

in its core. If you want to live a life of calling, you must listen to your pain. It will provide you with purpose. Listen to your suffering. It will speak of your significance.

If you listen, you will hear your calling.

Build Your Confidence

When we identify our future calling and reflect on what we've survived, we'll build confidence to withstand more challenges. We learn this in Romans 5, where the apostle Paul reminds us that struggles produce endurance, character, and hope (Romans 5:4)—everything we will need to face our next hardship with more resilience.

You've survived so much. You have faced difficulties and emerged stronger. Your faith has been forged in the fire because your God has shielded you from the flames. With God by your side, you can be strong and courageous. He has been with you in the past, and he isn't going anywhere now. He will never leave you nor forsake you.

When you align your present calling with past perseverance, you'll build confidence.

Two Important Clarifications

Before we move on, let me share two crucial clarifications.

1. Confidence cannot be in yourself alone; it must be in Christ. Some people who exude confidence have no reason to be so self-assured. Some people have a lot going for them but still lack confidence. You may or may not be a talented person. You may or may not have overcome great hardship in the past. But in either case, at some point, life is going to come at you so viciously that you won't have what it takes to fight back. You won't be able to charm your way out, power your way out, manipulate your way out, or even buy your way out. At some point, you won't have the answers, the cure, or the connections to escape. When that happens, your confidence will be in the toilet, and you'll become insecure and either quit or sabotage yourself.

Providentially, where you are lacking, Christ is abundant. And he is graciously willing to give strength where you are weak. His grace is sufficient. He delights in being there for you. He faced the one thing no one on earth is able to escape, and he emerged victorious. He has overcome death. If he is for you, who or what can be against you (Romans 8:31)? The path you're on may not be the path you wanted, but you can count on Jesus to be with you all the way through. When you can't count on yourself, you can find confidence in Jesus. Don't make Jesus your last resort when you can't find confidence in yourself; make him your starting point for confidence.

2. Calling is always placed in your life to bring about Christlikeness in your character. We must understand that calling is not always placed in your life for you to do great things. Narcissists and spiritually immature people often get distracted by chasing the idea that they are chosen for greatness. Most often, the calling of God doesn't have much to do with what we're doing, but rather has everything to do with who we are becoming. It isn't so much about what God is doing through you, but rather is doing in you. I've had up-close experience with how God's calling can cause character growth. I believe wholeheartedly that God will use everything that happens in our lives to help us look and act more like Jesus. One aspect of Christlikeness is being resilient. We can become more resilient people.

Living Your Calling

When confidence and calling collide, you find resilience, strength, and victory. It is then that you can live a purposeful life—a life rooted in your calling. Instead of running from obstacles, you can confidently face them and discover the rich opportunities waiting for you. As soon as you decide to identify opportunities from the obstacles you face, you'll begin to live with a particular calling on your life. Throughout your lifetime, you will face different obstacles and respond to different unique callings. As seasons of life change, so will your callings. One thing will remain constant: you can be a resilient person who has a calling on your life. As the apostle Paul writes, "I urge you to live a life worthy of the calling you have received" (Ephesians 4:1).

You aren't as strong as you think you are, but you are stronger than you ever could dream. The power of God's Spirit will transform your weakness into strength. Once you embrace this truth, you will stand on a rock-solid foundation that will not let you fall. When you bring together true confidence and a clear calling, you will finally find, deep within yourself, resilience, strength, and spiritual victory—and you will need it.

You will face times in your life when you will need to dig deep to continue moving forward. What does it mean to *dig deep*? I know from personal experience that it doesn't mean "giving it all you've got" or "trying harder." As I trained every morning for IRONMAN, I would pray the same prayer: *God, give me strength.* This simple prayer allowed me, in my toughest moments, to gain access, deep in my soul, to a dynamic spiritual strength. Once connected to the strength God supplies, a reaction of resilience occurs. It starts with strength of soul, which provides mental strength, and then supplies the strength to act. This is what it means to *dig deep*. In order to not give up, you must reach all the way into your soul.

Denial Is Devastating

When you get hit hard and knocked down, don't give up; get up. But be smart, and stay down for a period of time. Let yourself feel the pain. Identify what happened. Put words to the pain; name the emotions you are feeling. Count the cost, and be brave enough to come to terms with how much the knockdown could set you back.

Assess the damage. Whether the damage is physical, financial, or emotional, you must make a fair assessment before getting up and moving on. The results could be devastating if you don't.

Imagine being a college football player who went down hard after getting chop-blocked by a three-hundred-pound offensive lineman. It would be foolish to struggle back to your feet before the team doctors arrived and assessed your condition. To get back up before determining the damage could exacerbate a minor injury, turning it into a career-ending injury. It is the same with all sorts of life's hardships. If you get up before working through the pain, you risk compounding the immediate pain with long-lasting, traumatic effects—emotional, relational, and physical.

However, if you don't get up in due time, you might prolong the pain and sacrifice the potential opportunities awaiting you. Many people assess the damage and then dwell on the negative facts and feelings. They keep their faces planted in the dirt, even when it is time to raise their heads and get back on their feet.

You must take the time to feel the pain. Then when you've processed the loss, you must get up, even when you feel too weak to even try. In faith, make the first move toward standing—and that's when the Spirit of Jesus responds by strengthening your feeble limbs.

| Get Knocked Down | > | Feel and Assess the Pain | > | Get Up | > | Stay Strong and Press On |

Trying to move through the process too quickly can be damaging. Feeling and assessing the pain can be scary. You must courageously approach the negative emotions that come with your pain. The emotions are only temporary, which lets you feel them without being overwhelmed by grief. If you move too quickly and try to get up immediately after getting knocked down, the pain you ignore can stay with you for much longer than necessary. If you overspiritualize your circumstances, your denial can lead to great disappointment. Although painful emotions will make you feel weak, I promise you that you are strong enough to bear their temporary weight and still have the stamina to move on.

Here are four ways we often engage in denial to our detriment:

1. **Focus only on the spiritual and deny the scientific reality.** When you overspiritualize your life, you sabotage yourself. It takes courage to look at the facts. I've found it helpful to first make peace with the prognosis given by medical professionals—without giving up the hope of what God has planned for my life.

2. **Focus only on scientific predictions and deny the possibility of divine intervention.** It is helpful to look at reality without letting go of the very real possibility that God is powerful enough and compassionate enough to intervene and change the course of nature. Hope can be scary, but it is also powerful.

3. **Get too busy for grief.** If you find yourself being busier than necessary, take a step back and ask yourself if there may be some kind of loss that needs to be grieved. Whenever an abrupt change takes place, things that are lost need to be grieved. Without taking the time to grieve, you will be held back.

4. **Pay homage to the Friedrich Nietzsche quote, "What doesn't kill me makes me stronger."** [2] This aphorism has become conventional wisdom and can sometimes keep us away from self-pity, but it can also prevent us from admitting just how hard life is at any given moment. The popular phrase "it is what it is" can have similar effects. Minimizing hardship can result in denial.

---

2. This quote appears in Nietzsche's book of aphorisms, *Twilight of the Idols*. Kelly Clarkson sings a version of this phrase in her song "Stronger."

Instead of going into denial, acknowledge your hardship and rejoice despite the difficulty. We have already discussed how the joy of the Lord is our strength (go back and read chapter 9 if you need to). That joy is crucial for finding resilience. If you want to be a resilient person, you must learn how to access the Lord's joy. But let me tell you a secret. We can't choose joy—even though an internet search will reveal many books titled *Choose Joy*, along with shirts, bracelets, and wall art featuring that phrase. The only problem is that choosing joy doesn't work.

It seems to me that what people really mean when they urge us to choose joy is that we should *practice gratitude*. Gratitude is a gateway to joy. In many circumstances, stopping and smelling the roses will help us be thankful. Being thankful could help us turn a frown upside down. Finding happiness in the details surrounding us may change our perspective and move us closer to joy. But when we're facing something that ruins not just our day but possibly our lives, choosing joy is not an option. The truth is, it's not in our power to become joyful. Achieving a delightful disposition of the soul is, in the end, not something we can do on our own. Let's be real, most of the time we're not mentally strong enough to command our downcast soul to change to a joyful spirit.

Fortunately, God has given us a gift that contains power enough to get the job done—the Holy Spirit. As described in Galatians 5:22, joy is one aspect of the fruit of the Holy Spirit. One of the benefits of embodying the Holy Spirit is reaping the fruit of joy. We may not be able to choose joy, but we can ask for it. Jesus promises in Luke 11:13 that our heavenly Father will give the Holy Spirit to those who ask him. Remaining in Jesus, communing with the Spirit, and asking for joy can bring about miraculously resilient results. Think about it. The same Spirit that enabled Jesus to endure the cross is also in you. The joy of the Spirit gave Jesus the strength needed to accomplish his calling. And so we take to heart the words of the author of Hebrews:

Let us run with endurance the race God has set before us. We do this by keeping our eyes on Jesus, the champion who initiates and perfects our faith. Because of the joy awaiting him, he endured the cross, disregarding its shame. Now he is seated in the place of honor beside God's throne. Think of all the hostility he endured from sinful people; then you won't become weary and give up.

(HEBREWS 12:1–3 NLT)

The joy of the Lord that awaited Jesus was his strength at the cross. The joy of the Lord that awaits us is our strength as well. If you ask, God will use the joy of his Spirit to fuel your resilience.

When Faith Is Tested

Life is hard. Struggles and suffering threaten not only our quality of life; deeply difficult trials threaten our very faith. As a pastor, all too often I have seen hardships weaken people's faith, causing them to walk away from their faith altogether. Too many people walk away from the one source that can provide them with everything they need to persevere through difficulty. They so badly want to overcome in the face of adversity, but they walk away from the one who has already overcome the ultimate struggle.

Let me say to you that I want better for you. I want your faith to persevere. Life is stunning when you get to experience how God can use even the worst things for your good. Instead of being crushed beneath the weight of your trials, you can be strengthened by the weight of God's glory and emerge from the fire fortified with God's presence.

Cling to God and receive his blessing that turns your weakness to strength, transforms your character to look more like Christ, and increases your faith so you can become resilient. Then you will be a person of deep faith—never veering off the path, always persevering. Never wavering, always trusting. Gritty, determined, persevering, promise-keeping faith. You will be blessed, and you will bless the people you deeply love.

My victory was not at the IRONMAN finish line; my victory was at Dunkin'. When I first learned I had terminal brain cancer, it was at a donut shop that I faced the decision of whether to turn *to* God or *away* from him. That was where my faith was tested. What is your Dunkin'? After receiving my diagnosis and prognosis, I had to decide whether I would trust him to strengthen me so I could withstand the crisis or whether I would rely on myself. I decided in the parking lot of a donut shop to turn to God and put my faith in him. That's where I passed the test and experienced victory. From that point on, God carried me through cancer treatments and triathlon training. He was with me at the starting line and he stayed with me for the entire 140.6 miles to the finish line. And he is with me now. He is sustaining my life daily as I continue to battle a disease that has no known cure. He is my God, and I am his prized possession. He is with me and he is for me, and therefore I have no reason to fear. If I have anything of value to give you, it is this: turn to him. Trust Jesus with your life. He is trustworthy. I am a living testament to that.

If I can do it, you can do it.

Why and Yet

Knowing how to be resilient isn't enough; we need to know *why* we're choosing a resilient life. Knowing why an endeavor is worthwhile is the only thing strong enough to motivate us when we have nothing left. *Why* is the motivation needed for a resilient life. Having a compelling reason to persist can defy fear and defeat an overwhelming desire to give up and quit. A clear vision of what we hope to accomplish at the end of our endeavor can keep us on track. Our purpose can bring about persistence. However, our intention must be genuine. Setting a goal is not enough to inspire us to keep moving forward through the fire if our motive is not earnest and heartfelt. We must understand why we will press on.

You'll need to figure out on your own the reason for your willingness to stop at nothing and persevere through everything. Perhaps you could start here. You're breathing. Why? If you are still alive, you should be living. If you're still alive, God has a purpose and a plan for you to bless you—to prosper you and not to harm you (Jeremiah 29:11). God sustains your life. He is the author of your days. Your span of life is outside of your control. Stop trying to control everything. Don't save your life; spend it. What do you value most? Invest your life there.

You'll truly find something worth living for when you finally find something worth dying for. To the very end, spend your life on the things most valuable to you. Keep living to the very end. And when you feel like it's all too much and you're just too tired to go on, hear the Holy Spirit say to you, *Not yet, tired saint, not yet. You haven't come to the end yet.*

Yet is a powerful word. I think it may be the most resilient word ever written. To me, *yet* is a synonym for *resilience*. Embracing it will create a growth mindset. *Yet* holds the power to hold on for as long as needed. I was about 120 miles into IRONMAN and still had about twenty miles to go. I was in trouble. It seemed very likely that I wouldn't finish the race. I prayed the same prayer you would have prayed: *Help!* And nothing happened—yet.

Some of you just read that sentence and felt it in your bones. Sometimes you pray and nothing changes—yet. But hold on to that *yet* long enough, and it can become a yes. By the sustaining and sufficient grace of God, at the right moment, the *yet* becomes a *yes* and nothing becomes something. You prayed, *Help!* and yes, something happened. For me, I prayed, and nothing changed for the next ten miles—and then it did. By the grace of God, I crossed the finish line. When I started this ridiculous quest, I wasn't even a triathlete; now I'm an IRONMAN. I wasn't an IRONMAN—*yet*. Now I am.

It doesn't matter what you are not at this moment in time. You can become. You *are* becoming. If you want to gain more resilience, just add the word *yet* to your reflections. I'm not very resilient—yet. Things aren't coming together—yet. I'm not strong—yet. I'm not finished—yet.

I didn't give up all hope when I learned I had a terminal disease for which my neuro-oncologist told me there wasn't a cure—*yet*. She told me it was her job to keep me alive long enough for a cure to be found. I stopped praying just for myself and started praying for the researchers . . . and in effect, I was praying for the healing of *all people* who were suffering with my disease. The word *yet* inspired me to start praying bigger and living for something bigger than myself.

I didn't lose my faith when Jesus said no to my request for healing because I figured Jesus wasn't necessarily saying a firm and final no but was quite possibly saying, *Not yet*. Is it possible that just as Jesus first forgave a paralytic man's sins before healing his legs, could he be healing my heart before my physical health? Is it possible that I have not yet completed my ultimate calling? The possibilities are enough to give me hope that springs up out of my faith. It is enough to generate a million reasons why I shouldn't give up.

What are *your* reasons?

I do not have an iron will, but I have the strength of the Spirit.

---

*If you face your biggest obstacle head-on, you
will find your greatest opportunity to leave
your mark of love in the name of Jesus.*

---

1. In which of life's circumstances can you clearly see
    that you don't have enough willpower to persevere?

2. Reexamine the obstacles blocking your way. Is it
    possible that an opportunity is lurking that you
    haven't seen before? What hasn't happened for
    you . . . yet? How do faith and hope play into your life
    right now?

3. What in your life is worth living for? What is worth
    dying for? Resilience requires a *why*. What is your
    why?

CHAPTER 12

What and Why?

"Why do you call me good?"

JESUS (MARK 10:18)

What is true strength? Why do bad things happen to

good people? I will spare you easy answers and placating explanations. Instead, let me pass on some hard-earned insights that have brought me peace. May God bless you with peace as well.

How We Know

Obviously, strength is more than "an ability to exert force or withstand force." Weakness is more complex than to be defined simply as "a scarcity of strength." To understand the true meaning of strength, we must experience it. To fully experience strength, we must travel through weakness.

Ever since my college days, my favorite Greek word has been *ginosko*. The word simply means "to know by experience." It refers to relational understanding. This is the kind of knowledge needed to know God. When we are connected to Jesus through his Holy Spirit, experiential knowledge transcends rational reasoning by carrying a deeper, mystical quality of wisdom that is beyond our grasp by any means other than personal encounter. The concept of *ginosko* adds another significant layer to the experiences of life. We are not passive observers being acted on by life; instead, we participate in life, learning and growing through the lessons we participate in.

Perhaps it's my longtime love of the concept of *ginosko* that brought me deep comfort when I asked God why he would not heal me of terminal cancer. God heard my prayer and directed me to 2 Corinthians 12:8–10. His Spirit gave me insight, and I knew that what I was about to experience would teach me the true meaning of strength and weakness. Although God did not heal me, he satisfied my soul with hope of the wonderful experiential learning of a crucial subject—what it means to be truly strong.

You can memorize the dictionary definition of strength, but it's not until you experience it in the classroom of life that you can truly grab hold of all its vast intricacies. To my surprise, I discovered that to experience genuine strength, you must first travel through weakness. Weakness first, then strength. Strength is best experienced and most easily defined through weakness.

Foil

Weakness by definition is the opposite of strength. However, weakness is not strength's enemy. It is strength's counterpart that complements strength's complexity. Weakness draws attention to strength's commendable qualities.

My wife, Natalie, is a literary scholar. One day, we were talking about the interplay of strength and weakness, and she mentioned foil-backed gemstones. These precious gems are backed with cheap foil—a technique that began as far back as 2000 BC and reached its zenith in the 1800s. As light reflected off the foil, the quality of the prized jewels would be accentuated. In the same way, God's light reflects from our fragility and weakness to display his strength at work within us.

We get our modern literary definition of *foil* from jewelry making. In literary terms, *foil* is the character that enhances the qualities of the main character by contrast. Therefore we can say that weakness is a foil to strength.

In *The Lord of the Rings*, Frodo Baggins is the protagonist—the main character—of the story. Gollum is not the villain, enemy, or antagonist to Frodo. He actually serves as a guide for Frodo's heroic journey. Gollum also serves as a foil to Frodo. Author J. R. R. Tolkien included Gollum in the story to emphasize Frodo's virtuous qualities by way of contrast. In the same way, weakness accompanies strength when we walk any path of opposition. We cannot access strength without first passing through weakness. As Gollum is to Frodo Baggins, so weakness is to strength. Together, we see an incredible story.

Weakness shines a bright light on strength and puts its contrasting attributes on display. When a person is weak and yet is able to find the power to overcome adversity, that's when true strength becomes apparent and its origins are revealed. If you want to see strength illuminated in your life, look to your weaknesses. If you want to emphasize areas where you are already strong, lean into areas where you need to grow. Don't be surprised when you feel weak. It is an invitation to draw near to God, profess the frailness of your humanity, and ask for his divine strength to be transferred to your soul.

What Is True Strength?

Nearly two years before I crossed the IRONMAN finish line, I decided to do an experiment to test God's promise found in 2 Corinthians 12:8–10. If the Bible says that "when I am weak, then I am strong," what if at my weakest I attempted something that I did not believe

I could do in my prime? What would I discover about true strength and its source? As I reflect on the *ginosko* gained, here is what I know: true strength is of the soul, and its origin is the Spirit of Jesus. Strength is more than just muscle and might; it's endurance of faith to fight the good fight.

I do not have a new and improved definition of strength to offer. I don't believe strength can be defined in a single sentence. But I do have a few observations to offer that I hope will provide insight. Strength is forged in the flames of adversity. Strong people still stumble; strength arises out of struggle. Strength welcomes change despite pain; deep strength dynamically transforms hearts. Strength faces hardships with hope; strong people believe that where there are obstacles, there are also significant opportunities. Strength listens to calling and perceives purpose. Strong people find confident, consistent resolve that overcomes obstacles. Strength is that moment when you're scared but you face that fear and do the hard thing; it takes strength to find courage. Strength is love and takes love; deep love carries strength. Strength takes the first, uncertain step. Courageous people learn there is strength in the attempt. Strength looks meek; admitting weakness and accepting support is a strong move. Strength combines belief with purpose, providing a reason to persevere. Weakness is the beginning of all strength. First weakness, then strength.

Strength is spiritual. Inspiration instigates strength. Faith sustains strength while weak. Strength lets go of control while holding on to hope. Positive people remain resilient. Flexible people are resilient people, able to bounce back from disappointment. Strength forgives; strong people love people profoundly. Strength is heard in a simple, authentic prayer. Answered prayers provide power. Strength is renewed by grace; grace is powerful enough to satisfy the soul in times of suffering. Strength permeates to the core. Inner stamina has staying power. A resilient life is built on a resilient faith. Faith's foundations withstand imposing disasters. Strength is steady in the storm. Peace is the origin of unwavering endurance. Strength of soul stands firm. Solid conviction won't run from impossible problems. Strength is the decision to turn to God instead of blame God. Trust in God's character permits rest in crisis. Strength finds reason to rejoice even in the midst of suffering. The joy of the Lord is our strength (Nehemiah 8:10). God's power is best displayed through weakness (2 Corinthians 12:9).

I can personally testify that true strength is found in Jesus. He can move mountains, and he can provide the tenacity to climb them. Jesus delights in lending us his strength. He transforms our weakness to strength so that through him all things are possible. Jesus is not only strong; Jesus is strength. There is strength in Jesus.

Now that we've tried to define a concept as sophisticated as the word *strength*, let me ask a big question: *Why me?* Let's expand that question to become even more complex: Why do bad things happen to good people?

I don't know. I simply don't know why bad things happen to good people. And I am not so sure I'm a good person. Most people looking in from the outside might consider me a good guy. I'm a pastor. I try to be a good husband and father. I'm not involved with drug cartels. My lifestyle is socially acceptable by most standards. But hidden in my heart are many areas where I fall short and would be ashamed if you knew about them. I'm not alone in this. I don't think I deserve pain, but if pain is a reality in this world and is a part of the human existence, I don't feel like I'm so good that I should be spared.

The year I was diagnosed with a rare form of cancer, a multitude of other people received the same bad news as I did. In fact, if you got us all together, we could fill a sports arena. I'd wager to say that if we really did assemble together, I might find quite a few people who, by comparison, have more moral flaws than me—people who have done deplorable, disgraceful things. And I'm very sure many people in the arena would be considered saints when compared to me—those who have done more good, avoided more evil, and hid their secrets better than I have. You know the old saying: the sun rises and the rain falls on both the evil and the good.[1]

You can exhaust yourself trying to understand why some things are the way they are or happened the way they happened. Plenty of smart, godly people have dedicated their lives to studying the problem of evil and have written impressive books laying out their logical explanations. I have read some. Authors have made many good points, but none of them satisfy my soul. Nothing that I've read on this topic has brought peace to my heart and settled the question of why bad things happen to good people . . . or why God would allow evil at all. But one thing I have is my real-life experience. And it is more than anecdotal evidence. God has granted me *ginosko* as I have walked through the valley of the shadow of death. This experiential knowledge is necessary for any worthwhile contribution to the conversation on the purpose of the coexistence of good and evil.

I'd like to share the emotional, physical, and spiritual experience that has settled the storm in my soul. Maybe it will help you in your journey through life's ups and downs.

Why has God allowed me to suffer such a terrible evil? I have asked him this question, and he has not explained why. In the end, I don't really think my mortal mind could understand. Instead, God has answered with empathy. He has whispered to my spirit:

I AM WITH YOU.

I see you, and I feel you. I have been there. I came into the world and suffered the evil of the world.

I hate seeing you in pain. I hate the evil you are suffering. I will fix it.

I have paid the ultimate price to assure you that this pain is temporary. One day, I will welcome you home, embrace you, and

---

1. Matthew 5:45.

wipe away the tears with my nail-scarred hands. Until then, I will hear every cry and feel every pain.

I will be so close that I will feel even the emotion you can't put words to, and I will give it spiritual language.

I will redeem the evil done to you and will use it to give you great purpose in your life.

I will never leave you nor forsake you.

I AM WITH YOU TO THE END.

If you ask God, "Why me," he will answer, *Me too.*

You have a hard road to walk. So do I. So did Jesus. Even Jesus asked why. "My God, my God, why have you forsaken me?" he cried from the cross (Matthew 27:46). Although Jesus didn't hear his Father's voice in that moment, God was there, providing the strength Jesus needed to accomplish the most important mission imaginable. As Jesus suffered, God provided the wisdom and perspective to see the joy on the other side of the struggle. The joy of the Lord is strength. God provided him with enough strength to forgive the very ones who were taking his life, enough strength to say to them, "I forgive you; I don't blame you; I give my life for you." Suffering on the cross, Jesus did not abandon his faith in God's goodness because he was given the strength to trust that God had not abandoned him.

God Does Not Abandon

I don't need to know why. All I need to know is that God is good, that he cares about my pain, and that he will not abandon me. This knowledge brings peace to the raging storm in my soul. I have experienced what the Bible describes in Hebrews 4:15. Jesus really is an empathetic high priest. He understands my pain because he has experienced my pain—and worse. His empathy only bonds me to him. His grace is enough.

Many people in my situation walk away from their faith; they turn away from their God. In a very confusing, unfathomable time, I have made the decision to turn *toward* Jesus and not away from him. Every step of my incredibly difficult journey has been with Jesus, and he has provided exactly what I need to keep going.

Let me give you a tangible example. After I had gone to Dunkin' and asked God what he was doing and how I could cooperate—and receiving answers—I had another thing to figure out. What about my family? I had come to peace with my situation and felt a clear direction on what to do next. However, when a person gets sick, their concern is usually more about their family than themselves.

Where else could I turn than to God to air my concern for my family? I convinced a few friends to skip work on a Tuesday and come with me on a snowboarding trip to Mammoth Mountain. We left early in the morning and drove through the sunrise. We were among the first people to get on the chairlift. As the day developed, we were some of the only people who skipped work that day, leaving us to enjoy the perfect conditions with very few other people around. The runs were empty, covered with newly fallen powder on a sunny day. We had so much fun. It may have been one of the best snowboarding days ever.

We got so many runs in that by the end of the day, we were exhausted. We decided to do one more run before taking off. We had already hit every option down the mountain except for one. Earlier in the day, I had spotted a double black diamond (the most challenging runs on a mountain) near the bottom of the resort, which was weird. Most expert runs are at the very top, not the bottom, so I wanted to check out this curious route.

We started at the top and flew down the mountain together. But toward the bottom, my friends went right and decided to part ways and check out the run to the left. I soon learned why it was an expert run. It wasn't because of how steep it was; it was because it was a mogul run. The constant bumps can be a lot of fun for skiers, but they make for a lot of work without much payoff for snowboarders. But I was already committed, and I had to see it through.

After a long day, I was working really hard, throwing my board back and forth—so much so that the physical strain almost triggered a seizure. I felt myself getting light-headed. There was no one else in sight. I fully comprehended the danger of the situation, so I sat down and prayed I would be spared a seizure (which, thankfully, I was). As I sat on the side of the mountain catching my breath, I relaxed and looked toward the horizon. The surrounding mountaintops were all aglow from the setting sun. Thick white clouds surrounded one specific peak. The clouds were moving quickly, even though the air surrounding me was still. I sensed the presence of the Spirit and acknowledged the mystic environment I was in.

I took the opportunity to speak with God and discuss the thing most heavy on my heart. I prayed:

> *God, I'm good with what I am about to face. I can accept this path. But what about my family? What about Natalie? What about Hero? I know you're going to be with them in a general sense. But can I ask you for preferential treatment? Can I ask you to be especially close to them if my life is to end early? Can I ask you, like I would ask a best friend, to look after them? God, will you be there for them and look out for them? Like really, really look after them.*

In this prayer, I wasn't making requests; I was asking God something you would only ask your most trusted friend. I was asking him to take guardianship of my family.

God answered. He spoke what was nowhere near my mind at that moment: *That's why I sent you Peter Camarata. I sent him to you as a preview of things to come. I sent him to you to show you that I will continue to care for your family through my people, whether you're around or not.*

Let me tell you about Peter—a retired doctor in my church who volunteers in our children's ministry. He is every little kid's favorite, especially Hero. When Hero was six months old, she started having seizures, often while Natalie was holding her. This happened so many times that it traumatized Natalie. Can you imagine what it feels like to be a parent, holding your convulsing baby, helplessly waiting, not knowing what's going to happen, and not being able to do anything to stop it from progressing? During this time Natalie's anxiety skyrocketed.

Peter heard about what Natalie was facing and offered to be our personal pediatrician. He was just a phone call away and lived nearby. Whenever we were confused or scared about something, we called him. Often he'd come right over and usually tell us we had nothing to worry about. He always put us at ease and lowered our anxiety so we could enjoy Hero instead of being crippled with fear. We love Peter.

He is also a grandfather. He has the wisdom of an elder but has more energy than most twenty-year-olds. His wife died of brain cancer. After her death, his faith faded. But then he felt called to help me plant our church, and new life was breathed into his faith. He knows what it's like to be the spouse of someone with brain cancer. And he has great compassion for Natalie. He has already shown a great kindness to her, and I have no doubt he will continue to help her in any way he can.

Every conversation I have with him and every hug he gives feel so significant. He feels the same about us. Our family has always considered him to be a godsend. After my encounter with God, I realized that God indeed sent Peter to us. I believe that Peter is just the first of many godsends to follow. In fact, I can testify to an army of significant supporters who have rallied around my family since then. I asked God if he would take guardianship of my family. He didn't merely say yes; he said, *I already have.* And he would say the same to you.

Finish the Race

Endure in your faith. Where else could you go in your troubles than to Jesus, the Savior of God's children? He cares for you. Who else could you turn to than the one who walks with you in empathy and power? Trials will tempt you to abandon your faith, but I urge you to hang on. Join the apostle Paul, who at the end of his life was able to make this remarkable testimony:

> I have fought the good fight, I have finished the race, I have kept the faith. Now there is in store for me the crown of righteousness, which the Lord, the righteous Judge, will award to me on that day—and not only to me, but also to all who have longed for his appearing. **(2 TIMOTHY 4:7–8)**

People are inspired by my endurance. But it's not so much that I overcame hardship to finish an IRONMAN in the face of cancer. What leaves the biggest impression on people is my enduring faith in the face of uncertainty, tragedy, and the fulfillment of my greatest fear. This is not a testimony to my faithfulness; it is a testimony of the goodness of God and the strength he freely supplies. Who else could I want to turn to in times of trouble? He is my sanctuary, my rock, and my safe harbor. He will provide comfort, provision, and strength to whomever turns to him in times of trouble. If you are facing the unthinkable, you are not alone. You may not understand why, but try to imagine what it means to have God with you. Let the God of all empathy and power carry you. He will not only strengthen you, but he will also teach you the true meaning of strength.

Since being diagnosed, I've learned a lot. I have learned that strength that can bend steel, bench-press 225 pounds, or race 140.6 miles is superficial. To be sure, "physical training is good," but, as the apostle Paul went on to write, "training for godliness is much better, promising benefits in this life and in the life to come" (1 Timothy 4:8

NLT). The greatest strength in life is spiritual strength, and it is a strength that comes from weakness and fuels resilience.

Specifically, I have learned a superpower of godly strength—vulnerability. My spiritual training in the art of vulnerability has only begun, but even the initial progress I have seen in my spirit confirms that this is what I must give my life to—vulnerability that facilitates strong, significant connections with those I love the most: Natalie and Hero.

It is scary to put that in writing. This final chapter in my first book is now a contract between myself and Natalie and Hero. Only at the finish line of my life will they be able to determine if I've succeeded or failed. I have a lot to overcome. Everything in me tells me that showing weakness is a bad idea and that putting myself in vulnerable situations will only end in disaster.

So I'll need tons of intentional training. I will practice saying, "I'm scared. I was wrong. I need you. I messed up." I will take emotional risks, expose emotions I've been hiding, and learn to soften my countenance during conflict. I will have to drop the charade that I can do it on my own and don't need others. It's time for me to come close.

I modeled resilient faith to Hero from a distance. As Natalie pointed out on numerous occasions, it's time for me to disciple Hero shoulder to shoulder.

One night as Hero was falling asleep, she asked Natalie, "Do I have to do an IRONMAN to show someone I love them?" In typical Natalie fashion, she fielded that delicate question like a parenting pro, reassuring Hero that grand gestures are nice but that love is best shown through our consistent presence in the lives of those we love. Her explanation quieted Hero's heart and allowed her to fall asleep knowing she is greatly loved by both her parents and that she has the capacity to love others majestically and through the gift of simply sharing her life with others.

In every day I have left, I have the opportunity to model resilience for Hero. For it is in the often-mundane moments of life that we make our most lasting impacts.

After some time had passed since giving Hero a motivational speech at the finish line, I asked her, "What was your favorite part of the IRONMAN race."

Surprisingly, and without hesitation, she responded, "Getting that journal from you."

"Really?" I asked.

"Yeah, I love getting presents."

"Ah, that makes sense."

At the finish line, I gave Natalie a kiss and a bouquet of flowers. Hero got a speech and a journal. (I had bought one for myself too.) Just what every kid wants—thanks, Dad! It's a journal with fun activities and prompts that promote a *growth mindset* in kids. Since finishing the race, Hero and I have had jillions of daddy-daughter dates on which we do something adventurous and spend time working on the journal. This is one of the ways I'm intentionally pulling close to her and cherishing the time we have together. She loves it so much that she'll now ask out of the blue to work on the journal.

From up close, I see it building on the example I set from afar. Hero has already had to deal with more adversity than any little kid should. But I am so proud of her heart and can clearly see God's power working in her life as he builds a strong leader for future generations.

It's time for me to hold Natalie close and turn toward her even when I may be embarrassed by my vulnerability. I can no longer deny that I am weak. And I now have every reason to believe that when I am weak, then I am strong. I know full well that vulnerability and emotional connection will take far more strength and resilience than IRONMAN. Natalie deserves to feel profoundly loved as I open myself up enough to be available for her. It's time to turn my full attention to cherishing her and enjoying deep connection with the person who means everything to me. It's time to step up, stay strong, and press on to the end.

Full of Hope

I know what the medical community predicts about when and how my life will end. I have made peace with that possibility. I recently went to a memorial service of a pastor a few years older than me who died of brain cancer. I listened to his wife and daughter speak about him from the stage with tears in their eyes and sobs in their speech. I know this may be my path as well, but it doesn't have to be.

There is a hope in my heart that is undeniable. My hope is in God. He alone has the power to sustain my life. At some point, my life will come to an end, just as one day your life on earth will end as well. But God is the author of my life. Even if I don't get exactly what I'm praying for, I have absolute certainty that God will bring good things from this—and that gives me great hope.

I have seen God work miracles in my life and even greater miracles in my soul. I am now praying in expectation of a third miracle. I and many others are asking God for complete healing of this brain cancer that has no cure currently. We ask that God will sustain my life well beyond the prognosis I've been given. If this book has blessed you, will you bless me by praying for my healing? It's not that I believe if I get a certain number of people to pray for me, God will be forced to listen and grant my prayer. What I do believe is that the more people who are praying for me, the more glory God will get when he answers. So far his answers aren't what I have expected, but they have been good. What comes next I do not know. But I am full of hope, and my prayers are full of trust and positive anticipation—because I know who it is that I'm speaking to.

Now to him who is able to do immeasurably more than all we ask or imagine, according to his power that is at work within us, to him be glory in the church and in Christ Jesus throughout all generations, for ever and ever! Amen. **(EPHESIANS 3:20–21)**

FOR REFLECTION

To fully experience strength, you must travel through weakness.

You can know the dictionary definition of strength, but it's not until you experience it in the classroom of life that you can truly grab hold of all its vast intricacies.

1. Where are you taking shortcuts to try to avoid vulnerability? Are those shortcuts taking you off the path of building the strength needed to live a resilient life?

2. What key lessons are you learning as you experience difficulties?

Epilogue

The most transformational prayer I've ever prayed was the first prayer I had ever prayed. I was fourteen years old. My life was headed in a dangerous direction, and I knew it. I had just heard for the first time the good news of Jesus. And I responded by praying to God and saying, *If you were willing to die for me, I guess I can trust you. Take my life, and please teach me how to live it. I obviously don't know how.*

That moment drastically changed my life for the better. If your life feels out of control, the best move you can make is to entrust it to Jesus—the only one who is truly in control. If you feel all alone as you walk a difficult path, the most reliable person you can turn to is Jesus. This may be your moment—the moment when you put your faith in Jesus. He will walk with you. You can lean on him and trust that he will always be there for you—now and for eternity. That decision is yours and yours alone. But I can tell you, it is my faith in Jesus that has made me strong, just as he is strong.

Ever since I've followed Jesus, I've made it my aim in life to look more like him. Only now, at forty years old, have I recognized that Jesus is the embodiment of strength out of weakness and worthiness out of vulnerability. He was born into weakness—impoverished, displaced, completely dependent on others. But he grew into strength—engaged in a powerful ministry, confronting corrupt religious leaders, changing people's view of God, defeating death, setting God's children free. Jesus traveled through weakness to strength. His vulnerability emphasized his worthiness.

Just recently, I was reading through the last book of the Bible—the book of Revelation. In chapters 4 and 5, a scene is depicted in which the angels declare who is truly worthy in the kingdom of heaven—the Lord Jesus. Let me give you some snippets from a long passage to paint the picture of Jesus—who is as strong as a lion and as weak as a lamb led to the slaughter. Jesus is proclaimed to be strong because he subjected himself to weakness. He is counted worthy because he made himself vulnerable. Visualize with me this scene in the kingdom of God:

> I saw a strong angel, who shouted with a loud voice: "Who is worthy ... ?"
>
> "Look, the Lion of the tribe of Judah, the heir to David's throne, has won the victory. He is worthy...."
>
> Then I saw a Lamb that looked as if it had been slaughtered.... And they sang a new song with these words:
>
> "You are worthy ...
> For you were slaughtered, and your blood has
> ransomed people for God
> from every tribe and language and people and nation." ...
>
> Then I looked again, and I heard the voices of thousands and millions of angels around the throne and of the living beings and the elders. And they sang in a mighty chorus:
>
> "Worthy is the Lamb who was slaughtered—
> to receive power and riches
> and wisdom and strength
> and honor and glory and blessing."

And then I heard every creature in heaven and on earth and under the earth and in the sea. They sang:

> "Blessing and honor and glory and power
> belong to the one sitting on the throne
> and to the Lamb forever and ever."
> **(REVELATION 5:2, 5–6, 9, 11–13 NLT)**

I was struck by one contrast I had never noticed before. A mighty angel starts the conversation by asking who in heaven is ultimately worthy. The other angels point to Jesus, the Lion. But when Jesus appears, he does not look like the all-powerful Lion of God. Instead, he looks like the vulnerable Lamb of God—so weak that the people of the world could overpower him and slaughter him. But Jesus' real power is found in how he took the evil done to him and redeemed it for the ransoming of the children of God. It is his strength that came from weakness and vulnerability that has made him worthy of blessing, honor, glory, and power. So now I must also embrace my weakness and recognize that my vulnerability does not make me repulsive to God, but rather worthy in the kingdom of heaven.

When I put my faith in Jesus, I never asked for or expected an easy life. I wanted a life that matters. And now at my weakest, I have the greatest opportunity to make an impact on the people I love. When I look back on my calling at the age of seventeen to become a pastor, it was in reality a calling to tell stories of God's goodness. As I said before, God gave me a gift to tell stories, and now he has given me a story to tell. And my story is not done. Neither is yours. May God bless you with strength that follows weakness. May he use your vulnerability to build a resilient faith that fuels a resilient life.

Be blessed, my friends.

Acknowledgments

This is scary. I'm afraid I'll leave someone out. So many people have poured into me, in so many ways. Without them all, this book would not have been possible. Now here I am, scared to conclude this book. Talk about feeling weak! Haha.

Natalie and Hero. You are my reason for pressing on to make it home again. Your support in my medical fight, athletic endeavors, and writing this book has carried me. Natalie, thank you for taking a lot of time off work, making medical trips to San Francisco fun, worrying in waiting rooms, relocating to Houston, shouldering stress, and loving me in sickness and in health. Hero, thank you for being precious, resilient, caring, fun, brave, and inspiring.

Lisa Kirkland, Chris, John, Dean, and Drake—you were proud of me, and I needed that. Seeing you at the finish line will always be a cherished moment, second only to seeing you at the starting line of this whole fiasco at my surgery.

Charlie and Nancy Harris; Julie, Jason, Ben, Olivia, and Claire Cote—I married into a great family. I love you guys. Dave and Nancy Foster—you saved my life and will forever be true family.

Joosung and Imogen Fitz-Kwon—you were the first people to believe that this story was meant for more than just my family. Thank you, Joosung, for relocating from London to Orange County to capture this on film. *Dear Hero*, the feature documentary you created, so beautifully captured the images to these words and will forever be a treasured gift to my family and to anyone who watches the film. (P.S. *Dear Hero* is set to stream on Amazon Prime Video at the same time this book releases.)

To my agent, Greg Johnson of WordServe Literary—it's still hard to believe I have a literary agent. You took a chance on me, wrote an elegant letter to publishers, and convinced Zondervan to take a risk with me. Then you stood by me as a rookie and guided me through this wonderfully unknown process. I truly value your expertise.

Jim Burns of HomeWord—thanks for introducing me to your agent. I know it was a big ask. Carlos Whittaker—even in your busyness, you jumped on a phone call and bluntly said, "You need to write a book." Then you compellingly told me why. If it wasn't for you, this book would not be out in the world.

As I have already written, strength looks meek. Admitting weakness and accepting support are strong moves that have been difficult for me to make. Thank you, Connie Schwab, for listening to the prompting of the Holy Spirit and sending me the pivotal text message that emboldened me to share my burden and accept help from those who love me so very much.

When I was lost and needed someone in my corner, Kevin Crampton, you stepped in. We will be brothers forever. Cody Crampton, spending the day together at Disneyland was so helpful. Thank you for showing me the ropes.

Dr. Berger, to me you are the G.O.A.T. Your skillful surgeon's hand not only removed a life-threatening tumor from the middle of my brain, but you also saved my ability to move and access language. Needless to say, and quite literally, I would not have been able to write this book without you.

I had no idea what I was doing, but you, Margaret Hepworth, graciously gave me your time and prowess, both as an elite IRONMAN athlete and a breast cancer survivor. Your coaching got me to the starting line. Then you showed up for me and saved my race. Your caring heart got me to the finish line.

"One Arm" Willie Stewart—IRONMAN attracts inspiring athletes, among whom you are matchless. You networked on my behalf and garnered the support I needed.

I want to acknowledge and thank so many who trained with me and were with me at the race. Brad Stanfield drove an hour each morning to make sure I didn't skip the gym while I was suffering through radiation and chemo. Bill and Dee Peterson were a sensational tag team. Bill taught me how to ride a bike while Dee taught Hero to read and write as her personal tutor while schools were shut down due to COVID-19. Travis Rudd left work early every day to teach me how to swim. Erik Wakeling swam with me in open water to keep me alive and showed me that even pastors can attempt IRONMAN.

Support from my community was consistent throughout this journey, especially on race day. Brittany Brechwald produced all the details. From the seaside wedding venue gazebo for the opening ceremony, to the forty aid stations staffed with one hundred volunteers, to the fully lit finishing structure with a red carpet that approached the official IRONMAN tape—she is simply amazing (also, I can't imagine what it was like to try to get all those people who were crammed into the finishing area to keep their masks on, haha!). Steve Carter jumped on a plane to host the opening ceremony and rally everyone around me in prayer. At the start of the race, Brian Wurzel kept it light and made me laugh. Kane Johnson, Jon Ankenman, and Corrie Matson staffed a chase vehicle and stayed with me all day to provide medical and mechanical assistance if needed. Patrick Thayer coordinated all the law enforcement efforts and escorts. Jon Juroe handled the big-time construction needs.

I am blessed to still be experiencing consistent support from my faith community. Every pastor needs a pastor outside of their own church. Joe Grana, you've been my pastor for a long time. In the pure sense of the word, you are the best pastor I know. Matthew Cork, you too are my pastor, but you are also my boss. Fortunately for me, you are a good boss and a great friend. You dropped everything to fly five hundred miles to be there for me at my surgery. I am grateful you were there, laughing with me right before surgery, and still there with me now that I've returned to work. The space you have given me to share this God-story is a testimony to your incredible leadership.

To the team at Zondervan—not only did you take a risk on signing me, but you also provided an amazing team to make this project succeed. Each of you is incredible, and I thank God for you. I never expected a publisher would believe in me wholeheartedly and be so excited for this book to be released. You blow me away.

I'd like to thank any reader who made it this far. You are a special kind of person if you read the acknowledgments, and I love you for it! Thanks for reading. I am praying now as I write that this book has blessed you, inspired you, and brought you hope and strength.

Ultimately, I thank Jesus. My aim is that this entire book is a testament to the goodness of my God. Jesus, I love you, and I will always turn to you. Where else would I go?

Appendix

22 PROVERBS OF STRENGTH IN WEAKNESS

Strength cannot be defined in a single sentence, but I believe we can gain insight into its reality as we meditate through prayer. Slow down, take a deep breath, and consider what true strength looks like and how it is experienced. Read slowly through these twenty-two proverbs of strength, and ask the Spirit of Jesus to enlighten your soul and strengthen you to the core of your being.

1 Strength is forged in the flames of adversity. > Strong people still stumble; strength comes from struggle.

2 Strength welcomes change despite the pain. > Deep strength dynamically transforms hearts.

3 Strength faces hardships with hope. > Where there are obstacles, there are significant opportunities.

4 Strength listens to calling and perceives purpose. > Confident, consistent resolve overcomes obstacles.

5 Strength is that moment when we're scared but we do it anyway. > It takes strength to find courage.

6 Strength is love and takes love. > Deep love carries strength.

7 Strength takes the first, uncertain step. > There is strength in the attempt.

8	Strength looks meek.	Admitting weakness and accepting support are strong moves.
9	Strength combines belief with purpose.	Having a reason to persevere sustains strength while weak.
10	Strength lets go of control while holding on to hope.	Positive people remain resilient.
11	Strength forgives.	Strong people love people profoundly.
12	Strength is spiritual.	Inspiration instigates strength.
13	Strength is heard in a simple, authentic prayer.	Answered prayers provide power.
14	Strength is renewed by grace.	Grace is powerful enough to satisfy the soul in times of suffering.
15	Strength permeates to the core.	Inner stamina has staying power.
16	A resilient life is built on resilient faith.	Faith's foundations withstand imposing disasters.
17	Strength is steady in the storm.	Peace is the origin of unwavering endurance.
18	Strength of soul stands firm.	Solid conviction won't run from impossible problems.
19	Strength is the decision to turn to God instead of blaming him.	Trust in God's character permits rest in crisis.
20	Strength finds reason to rejoice even while suffering.	The joy of the Lord is strength (Nehemiah 8:10).
21	Weakness is the beginning of all strength.	First weakness, then strength.
22	God's strength is best displayed through weakness.	When you are weak, then you are strong.

From the Publisher

GREAT BOOKS

ARE EVEN BETTER WHEN THEY'RE SHARED!

Help other readers find this one

- Post a review at your favorite online bookseller

- Post a picture on a social media account and share why you enjoyed it

- Send a note to a friend who would also love it—or better yet, give them a copy

Thanks for reading!